FROM HANDEL TO HALLÉ

Professor Herkomer, 1890.

FROM HANDEL TO HALLÉ

Biographical Sketches

BY

LOUIS ENGEL

WITH AUTOBIOGRAPHIES OF

PROF. HUXLEY AND PROF. HERKOMER

Essay Index Reprint Series

BOOKS FOR LIBRARIES PRESS
FREEPORT, NEW YORK

First Published 1890
Reprinted 1972

Library of Congress Cataloging in Publication Data

Engel, Louis.
   From Handel to Hallé.

   (Essay index reprint series)
   Reprint of the 1890 ed.
   CONTENTS: Handel.--Gluck.--Beethoven. [etc.]
   1. Musicians--Biography. I. Title.
ML385.E57 1972   780'.92'2 [B]   72-854
ISBN 0-8369-7312-7

CONTENTS.

LIST OF ILLUSTRATIONS.

PREFACE.

THE very kind way in which public and press have received my last book, "From Mozart to Mario," encourages me to hope that similar indulgence may be extended to the present effort. There are a few essays in this volume which have been already published in a magazine, others are new ; two however, for which I need not ask any leniency, are autobiographies, and when I mention the eminent names of Professor Huxley and Professor Herkomer, I think it will be sufficiently clear that if I do not especially recommend them, it is because the interest which they cannot fail to awaken renders leniency unnecessary.

That scientific giant, Professor Huxley, everybody knows, need only put his pen to paper to command general attention, while the autobiography of Professor Herkomer is the most straightforward, and in its simple honesty, one of the most remarkable products of the kind, I ever remember having seen in print. As a painter, as a master, as a lecturer, and lastly as a musician, he tells you his successes with the ingenuity of a child, and without being wanting in modesty, he has the self-consciousness of genius, and in the simple words, "This was another of the arts I had to find out for myself," he shows you in a few outlines what the expression, "a self-made man," really means.

It will thus be seen that I have very little merit myself in the success of this book, should it be so fortunate as to meet with success. Yet the difficulty of getting correct information concerning details of the lives even of the greatest men must not be underrated. This desire to find out, and the still more dangerous proceeding to say, the truth is well represented in the French proverb : "*La vérité se trouve au fond d'un puits —faut être un sceau* (sot) *pour l'aller chercher.*" (The pun lies in *sceau*, bucket, and *sot*, idiot). I believe that I can safely say that there is not likely to be found an untrue word in this volume. How far it may interest, amuse, or instruct the reader, I must leave to my wise judges to decide.

In one respect I believe the reader will be satisfied : that is, the manner in which the publisher has done his work. There is an unpublished letter and a musical MS. of Beethoven exactly reproduced. The portraits have been engraved from the most reliable sources, and among others I think that the portrait of Madame Patti, for instance, at the age of seven years, has never been published ; yet the child's face is so entirely that of the great prima donna, that it cannot for one moment be mistaken. And now let me hope that with the art and help of others, my feeble essay may find a chance to please you.

L. ENGEL.

LONDON, *Easter*, 1890.

𝕳andel,

HIS EARLY YEARS.

FAIRY tales are bound to begin with: " There was once upon a time a fair princess with golden hair and violet eyes," etc. And if you do not begin in this strain you revolt against the tyrant of life, habit. Children will not be told a story unless it is told in this fashion. Big children will not be told a biography or even a sketch of a great man's life unless it begins thus: George Frederic Handel was born in the year 1685, on Feb. 23. He would therefore be two hundred and four years old if he was now alive. Unfortunately, however great a man may be, he sometimes dies before such an age can be attained. Handel's birthplace was Halle, in Saxony; his father a surgeon was sixty-three years old when he was blessed by the birth of our hero. Strange to say nothing was more distasteful to the old gentleman than music, and, terrified to discover that his little boy, as he grew up showed a strong inclination for music, he resolved to resort to the most stringent measures to keep all music and musical instruments out of his son's way, and rather prevent his going to school, that he should not be taught music there. The unusual energy and inflexible will for which Handel was well known in after

life showed themselves, however, in his childhood, for
when he was but seven years old he contrived, by the
help of his mother and a friendly nurse, to get a little
harpsichord up a garret in his father's house there to
practise all to himself.   Again, when his father refused
to take the child with him on a journey to an organist,
a son of a previous marriage, the little boy watched for
the departure of the carriage, and running by a short
cut, contrived to overtake the vehicle, and so earnestly
begged his father would allow him to share his company, that he gained his object and was permitted to
travel with his parent.   The relative they were going
to see, being in the service of the Duke of Saxe-
Weissenfels, little George was admitted to the service
in the private chapel, where he found means to creep up
to the organ and in his own fashion to play so originally
that the Duke's attention was drawn to him, and so
amazed was he to see a mere child organist that he sent
for the father and there and then overcame the surgeon's
determination to make a lawyer and not a musician of
his son, and from that moment Handel's regular musical
studies began.

I need not tell the intelligent reader that there is
nothing new to be said about so well-known a name as
Handel, but since an attempt has been made in so many
languages to write his biography, I hope that taking
the most interesting parts of each of them, I may be
able to give some facts as yet unknown in this country.
I cannot suppress the remark that while the Germans
are dreadfully particular as to completeness, and for that
purpose cram their books with innumerable and often

quite irrelevant details, yet it must be conceded to them, that what they do state as a fact, is a fact, and though they go into unnecessary depth and expand into unnecessary breadth, that which they say you can rely upon. Not so with French writers, less still with Belgians. I have seen a work on Handel by a Frenchman, published only a very few years ago, where in the most innocent manner the author declares that he writes a life of Handel, because "there is none to be found in French, English or German" ! ! ! And he calls his hero Frideric, probably to show that he will not use the French name Frédéric, but the German, which by-the-bye is Friedrich, so that Frideric is only so far justified that Handel himself sometimes amalgamated the French and German and signed " Friederic."

It is curious that Handel's father, after having married a widow more than ten years older than himself, a year after her death, when he was sixty-one years old married again. This second wife was twenty-eight years younger than he (33). Two years later she became the mother of George Frederic Handel.

The first works mentioned of Handel are ten sonatas for two hautboys and a bassoon. He was then ten years old, and one year after this his master, Zachau, declared to his father that although only eleven years old, he knew as much as his master and that he could teach him no more. Handel nevertheless continued studying and writing, copying old masters' works and learning from that exercise. He was then sent to Berlin, where he made the acquaintance of Buononcini, whom in later days he was to meet again in London and with whom he had the same troubles of competition, the same excitement in public and the same division of parties, *pro* and *con*, as in Paris had the Gluckists and Piccinists. This musical strife so enraged Addison that he ridiculed 'Rinaldo,' Handel's first opera given in London on Feb. 24th, 1711, Handel being then in his twenty-sixth year and having written the opera in *fourteen days*. Dean Swift's epigram anent the contentions between the two composers is well known :—

> " Some say that Signor Bononcini
> Compared to Handel is a Ninny,
> Whilst others say that to him Handel
> Is hardly fit to hold a candle ;
> Strange that such difference should be
> 'Twixt tweedledum and tweedledee."

Is it not very strange that about the same time Lessing, the great German poet (1729–1781), should have written very nearly the same kind of verses ?

> " Hilf Himmel welche Zänkerei
> Um Didldum und Didldei ! "

Having mentioned the opera 'Rinaldo,' which was sketched from Tasso's 'Gierusalemme liberata,' by Aaron Hill, director of the Haymarket Theatre, and retranslated into Italian by Rossi, I may as well say that the financial success of the opera was such, that Walsh, the music publisher, made £1,500 by the sale of it. When he wrote to Handel to be sure and let him have his next opera, Handel sent him the following witty reply :—" As it is only right that we should be upon an equal footing, *you* shall compose the next opera, and *I* will sell it."

Handel's father died when his son was twelve years old (1697), leaving twenty-eight grandchildren, and two great-grandchildren. In remembrance of his father's wish young Frederic studied law until his seventeenth year, when suddenly he took to travelling, saw Italy, composed there opera after opera, until, as we have seen, he arrived in London, and wrote his successful opera 'Rinaldo' here. That after the great sensation this work created many friends should have advised him to stay in England, is not surprising, but being under an engagement with the Elector of Hanover (afterwards George I.) he left, after having been received in audience by Queen Anne, who gave him valuable presents, and expressed a wish to see him again.

So in 1712 Handel returned to England. The Peace of Utrecht being concluded, Queen Anne commanded Handel to compose a Te Deum and Jubilate, and settled upon him an annual pension of £200. She died in August, 1714, and in September of the same year King George arrived in London, very cross with Handel for not keeping his word to return to Hanover after a "reasonable stay" in England, for such had been the condition of his second leave. But what is reasonable? You allow a man a reasonable income, and you may think that on five pounds a week a man need not starve. But there are people who consider it reasonable to take a daily drive in a carriage with four springs and two thoroughbred horses; and those will perhaps not go very far on five pounds a week. Handel thought it reasonable to stay as long as he liked, but being of very different opinion the King would perhaps never have

forgiven him, had not Baron Kilmansegg, a personal
friend, undertaken through a clever expedient to bring
about a reconciliation.   He caused Handel to write
some music to be executed during a water-party in a
barge following that of the King himself, which so enchanted the King, that he allowed the baron on a
subsequent occasion to bring Handel to court to accompany the great violinist, Geminiani, when he not only
forgave Handel, but settled upon him a pension of £200
in addition to the pension granted by Queen Anne.

It is true that Handel only wrote one work in German,
but not as has been alleged that he wrote only one
work in Germany, 'Die Passion.'   He wrote two operas,
'Almira' and 'Nero,' both performed in Hamburg
in 1705, when he was twenty years old.   He was so
independent that when his mother, who lived in Halle,
thinking that her boy (in 1703 eighteen years old) might
be in rather straitened circumstances, sent him, for
Christmas, a little money.   He by return of post sent
it back, adding even a little present, to show that he
was quite able to support himself.   I think I should
have mentioned that Handel called 'Almira' and
'Nero' "*Singspiele*," not operas : the German expression
just quoted corresponding with what the French call
opéra comique which is by no means necessarily a comic
opera, but an opera with spoken dialogue and no recita-
tives.   Great composers were at that time not overpaid,
and Handel, in 1705, and in both the preceding and
the following year, gave piano and harmony lessons for
one pound (sometimes for sixteen shillings) per *month !*
And from this scanty income he accumulated economies

to the tune of 1,000 francs (£40) in three years ; and thus was enabled to make the journey to Italy and hear what the musicians there could do. It is during his sojourn in "that blessed garden of Europe" that his double opera, 'Florimond and Daphne,' was given at Hamburg by the new manager Sauerbrey. Handel's journey to Italy was another proof of his independence, for Prince Gaston di Medici, brother to the famous Prince Ferdinando, offered to take him free of expense, but Handel refused, preferring to be his own master. I only just mention his quarrel with Matheson, which led to a duel with a harmless ending and reconciliation of the two friends, because it has been exaggerated into an attempted assassination. It was the same Matheson who travelled with him to Lubeck, where they competed for the place of organist, but when they heard that one of the conditions was that the successful organist had to espouse the daughter of the old organist they both fled, a sad compliment to the lady's charms.

Power of will is one of the principal qualities we have to look for in Handel. Is power beauty, as strength is grace ? It may be in some sense, but certainly not always. For instance, Gilbert Duprez, the great French tenor, was in his voice as well as in his appearance a very model of power : short, thick set, as tenors so often are, he was created for the part of Samson, but as to his beauty, the following little story will enlighten the reader. Duprez once walked away from the Grand Opéra with the baritone, Baroilhet, who was not an Apollo either. Whom should they happen to meet but

Perrot, the dancer, a man of very great ability, but short and thin, and ugly to such an extent that a manager, whom I do not wish to name, said to him he could never engage him unless for the Jardin des Plantes (zoological garden), as he engaged no monkeys. Perrot told them the story, and when Duprez laughed at him, Perrot said, " Why, surely you need not laugh ; if I am ugly, I am certainly not so ugly as either of you." " You monkey," said Duprez; "this difference shall soon be settled," and seeing a gentleman pass whom he had never known, but who appeared to be a well-bred man, "Monsieur," said he, "will you be so good as to make the umpire in a little difference of opinion between us?" " With pleasure," said the stranger, " if I can."   " Well," said Duprez, "just look at us, and say whom you consider to be the plainest of the three?"   The gentleman looked quietly and pensively for some time from one to the other, and then he said, " Gentlemen, I give it up ; I cannot possibly decide ! " and he went off roaring with laughter.

Handel's fame as an improvisator and clavecinist was such, that when he arrived in Italy and went *incognito* to Venice, that is, masked and disguised, to a fancy ball, the moment he played on the harpsichord, and Scarlatti heard him, he exclaimed, " This must be either the famous Saxon, or the devil himself." If improvising is composing, composing is with some masters of a genius comparable to that of Handel improvising : at any rate we cannot call composing in such rapidity otherwise. I mentioned ' Rinaldo,' but it is still more astonishing to learn that he wrote ' Israel in Egypt,' in my humble

HANDEL.9

opinion his finest oratorio, which is tantamount to saying the finest oratorio ever written, in twenty-seven
days, and the 'Messiah,' the world-famed 'Messiah,' in
twenty-three days! Taking into account the number of
choruses in the first-named oratorio, the mere rapidity
of committing so many notes to paper in the time, is
stupefying. And, will it be believed? 'Israel in Egypt'
failed entirely when first performed!

It is well known that Handel wrote the first part of
the 'Messiah' in seven days; the second in nine days;
and the third in six days; taking another day for
touching up the scoring, and he was fifty-six years old
then!

The beginning of the last century was the time when
Italy was thought the acme of civilization, the country
where alone you could study art in its highest cultivation
—music, poetry, painting, sculpture. Handel went in
the beginning of 1707 to Rome—he was then twenty-
two years old—to hear, just as young Mozart did when
a mere child, the famous 'Miserere of Allegri,' in the
Sistine Chapel, performed by the private singers of the
Pope. I do not know whether the ideas of people in olden
times were more restricted, and they were therefore much
less exacting and easier satisfied than our contemporaries, but I am bound to say that if the composition of
Allegri, and the singing of the castrati could give them
pleasure, they were not spoiled indeed. It does not
appear that Handel was very deeply impressed or inspired either by that music, for what he composed
during his sojourn in Rome belongs to the most in-
effectual part of his work. He was driven from Rome,

where he was imprudent enough to stay until the month of July, by the malaria and fear of fever.

He went to Florence, and this epoch of his life offers not only the interest that he there wrote his opera, ' Rodrigo,' but he seems to have made a most passionate impression on the heart of one of the most talented, amiable and handsome singers, Vittoria Tesi. Whether he responded in any measure whatever to that passion is not known, but it is certain that he had no serious thought in the matter, because he soon left for Venice, where he wrote ' Agrippina,' and when slyly questioned with regard to his ' Vittoria ' (victory), he answered (perhaps after him Beethoven) that the only woman he loved in this world was his Muse ! This opera ' Agrippina,' which had, what at the time was considered great success, viz., twenty-seven performances, was by some esteemed a noisy innovation, whereas the present publisher of Handel's works in this city perpetually adds brass to his scores. Mozart had done so for Handel in the last century, though he had been judged noisy before. So was Rossini called Il Signor Vacarmini. What would those good people have said could they have heard an opera of Verdi or Wagner ? For at a rehearsal of a Verdi opera it once happened that they had to stop a moment because the big drum could not go on without a little rest, whereas Wagner had a series of new brass instruments especially manufactured for his operas.

Handel returned after his Venice triumph to Rome, where he lived at the Marquis de Ruspoli's house, and there composed an oratorio, to which I wish to draw the reader's attention, for a particular reason. The name is

'La Resurrezione,' containing two superb choruses and arias, taken where from do you think? From his *opera* 'Agrippina.' Rossini said, "With regard to music, I know only two kinds: La bonne et la mauvaise." Of this opinion Handel must have been too, when you take into consideration the use he made of his 'Agrippina' airs.

Having for his librettists the Cardinals Ottoboni and Pamphili, it will readily be understood that he without difficulty gained the ear of the public. In that time, too, he wrote 'Il Trionfo del Tempo,' which is more a work of curiosity and interesting instrumentation than of commanding grandeur, and I only mention it because it is now understood to belong to his oratorios, whereas at the time it was called 'Serenata,' as it had not biblical words.

The French writer, whom I have quoted in the beginning of this sketch mentions a great *embarras* into which he fell whilst reading an English book. He says that he cannot make out the name of the Pope to whom Handel was introduced, as there is to his knowledge no Pope Gay in the world. The joke is that what the book says is that Handel lived for three years with Lord Burlington, and was there introduced to Pope, Gay, and Arbuthnot.

The unfortunate idea which has ruined so many people during both the last and the present century, the ambition to be appointed Director of the Italian Opera, seized hold of Handel, and it swallowed a fortune. To help him, the King was the first to contribute £1,000, but it cost Handel not only £10,000 (all his savings), but in order not to remain behind with the artist's salaries, he gave them bonds which afterwards were duly and honourably paid. Care and excitement led to a paralytic stroke, and he temporarily lost the use of one side. This is but natural with a man of his fiery temperament and over-heated blood.

Signora Cuzzoni, the great prima donna of his Opera troup, sent him once back an air which he had written for her, saying that she could make no effect with it. Handel, instantly enraged, is said to have run to her house with the manuscript in his hand, and—I will not vouch for the words—to have said to her, "You too, you will not sing my air—do I not know better what is good for you—you are the devil, but I am Beelzebub, the prince of devils, and I will vanquish you." Which saying, he caught Signora Cuzzoni round the waist, and being of proverbial Herculean strength, carried her to the window and shouted in infuriated tones, "You want a fresh air? I will give you fresh air, for if you will not sing my air as I wrote it, I will throw you out in the street from this window. Will you swear or not, you will sing?" I don't know whether prima donnas were spoiled at that time as they are now, but I scarcely imagine that to have been the right way to conciliate this one's friendship, for, at the first opportunity, when enemies and rivals of Handel's theatre founded another Opera in Lincoln's Inn Fields, Signora Cuzzoni remembering the fresh air he had made her take at the window, seceded and passed over to the enemy.

Without being overbearing, Handel knew his own value quite well. But as to proud self-confidence other great men, such as Beethoven and Victor Hugo, met in

a certain sense on the same path. The former committed somewhere what a small soul of a pedant pointed
out as a harmony mistake—consecutive fifths. "What
of it?" said Beethoven. "Fifths are forbidden? Well
then I permit them." In the same way Victor Hugo,
when reading a piece before the committee of the
Comédie Française, indulged in a phrase of not exactly
strict grammar. One of those insects whom nothing
makes so happy as to discover a mote in a friend's eye,
busily got up and said: "Would you mind one humble
observation, sir?" "What is it?" asked Victor Hugo,
with majestic superiority. "This phrase seems to me
not entirely French." "*Elle le sera,*" replied V. Hugo,
with the same pride as Beethoven.

Handel was what was then called a pianist, the condition of the instrument a hundred and thirty years ago
being rather restricted, and he was a great organist.
His proficiency on the organ must have been undoubtedly very great, because Domenico Scarlatti, the son of
the Great Alessandro Scarlatti, when asked by Cardinal
Ottoboni to play against Handel a sort of musical
duel, confessed that "he had not imagined that it was
possible for any man to play the organ as Handel did."
It is even said that whenever anybody complimented
Scarlatti on his organ playing, he invariably replied:
"What am I compared with Handel?" And devoutly
he crossed himself whenever he pronounced the name
of the *gran Sassone*.

I beg permission to diverge for a moment. We are
continually comparing our singers with those of the
grand old times, and we find that the eagerness to make

money, and to get that with all possible speed, prevents
our singers from studying so much as they did in the
last and in the beginning of this century. But without undertaking to explain the cause, the fact is that
voices such as they existed at Handel's time, cannot
easily be found now. Handel wrote in the well-known
'Acis and Galatea' for a singer who undertook the part
of Polifemo, containing an aria with an extent of *two
octaves and a fifth* : and in another air ('nell Africane
selve') even one whole tone more. When Handel gave
his opera 'Rinaldo' here, he inserted this grand air
of Polifemo, note for note, and made Signor Boschi,
for whom it was composed, come here from Naples and
sing it in the Opera.

It has often been asserted that Handel took other
people's melodies and gave them out for his own. Apart
from the slight objection to this assertion, viz. that it is
not true, there are some melodies which he has avowedly
taken, and those he has himself freely designated. 'The
Harmonious Blacksmith,' a series of variations on a very
simple *motif*, which he pretended to have heard a blacksmith singing when rain obliged Handel to seek shelter
in the workshop ; and the 'Pastoral Symphony' which
he put in his 'Messiah,' and which is a repetition of a
melody played on Italian bagpipes about Christmas
time, and which he indicated by writing over the melody
"Pifa," which means Pifferari, are among these.

Thomas Britton, a man to whom Handel was in the
habit of going to play the harpsichord and the organ,
before the famous beauty, the Duchess of Queensbury,
and a select circle of distinguished people, had been a

man who carried on his back small coal which he sold
in the street ; he by degrees increased his trade, and
taught himself without any help, to play the viol di
gamba, and the piano so well that the people ran to
hear him ; by-and-by several musical artists joined him,
Handel among others. He established a music-room
over his coal-cellar, by dividing it horizontally, leaving
the lower part for his trade and making the new ceiling
serve as the floor of his music-room, which was so low
that one could barely stand upright therein, and in that
locality the best society of London met the most distinguished performers of the day, and there it was that
the best music was heard. When the "small coal man"
died, he left a superb collection of MSS. and the two
instruments above mentioned. One of the most remarkable circumstances concerning this remarkable man,
was, that he, whose only portrait represents him with a
soft hat and a blouse, had numbers of friends and not
an enemy. How many patrons of art of the present
day can say as much ?

In a work published in 1799 a remark occurs which
we might copy to-day with equal propriety. "Italian
opera," says the author of ' Anecdotes of Handel's Life,'
"it is clearly ascertained, without considerable subscrip-
tions and strenuous exertions, can never be advanta-
geously maintained in London." This remark was
made when Handel was ruined the moment a rival opera
house was opened, while the other house did no good
business either. It has happened in London year after
year that the struggle of two, once even three, Italian
Operas, led only to the disaster of all concerned. It is,

therefore, not to be wondered at that Handel left opera composing altogether, and began the grand career in which he won immortal fame and glory—the Oratorio. And although he wrote his first oratorio in 1720, when he was thirty-five years old, and had already composed no less than forty-one operas, he wrote on to his sixty-sixth year, composing sixteen oratorios, which after nearly a hundred and fifty years still possess the greatest drawing power in our concert rooms.

I mentioned that Handel said he loved no female but the Muse. I am enabled, in the interest of truth, to maintain that, because, being a handsome man (usually the most important factor with marriageable ladies), and celebrated even in his youth, he came twice very near the sacred bond of marriage. Once a young lady, madly in love with him, told her father that, come what may, she would only marry this man and no other. Unfortunately the father in Handel's hearing declared that, so long as he lived, his daughter should not marry a fiddler. This word so exasperated Handel, that soon afterwards when the father died and the mother, who saw her daughter pine away, told Handel that all obstacles were now got rid of, he replied that all was over between her daughter and him, and he, "a fiddler," would have nothing to say to her. The poor girl died from a broken heart—a fact as rare as the phrase is frequent. The second opportunity was thrown in his way by a very rich lady, handsome and accomplished in every way—in fact a most desirable person ; but her family, although they had no objection to the man, insisted that he should give up his profession, a request which he proudly refused, preferring to live on his own earnings rather than on the wealth of a bride.

Perhaps I may be allowed here to allude to an absurd habit which consists in the title of Mus. Doc. being taken for a guarantee that the man on whom. it has been conferred must be not only a learned musician but a great composer. A great composer must be a great musician; but it does not follow that a great musician must be a great composer; for, a great musician is he who has learned all you can learn—thorough bass, harmony, counterpoint, composition. He will be pronounced a great musician if he offends against no rule, if, for instance, he can write an orchestral score and make no mistake, giving no instrument either notes or passages which it cannot play, violating no rule of harmony, etc.; but, just as a man can learn grammar, syntax, style, and, without offending against any rule, may not be able to write an interesting book unless he have ideas of his own or an original way of representing things as distinguished from the ordinary claptrap, so will no man write a great composition without new ideas of his own, or a style of his own. Being a musician is, in fact, a negative quality, not to make unallowed mistakes, just as a well-educated man will not offend against good manners; but being a great composer is an absolute merit. You must not only show what you don't do, but what you can do; you must create, you must give something that nobody before you has given, and though a doctor's diploma may prove that you have written a faultless MS., no title on earth can give you genius and make you a composer. A Welsh paper once distinctly

C

stated that Dr. P. stands higher than Beethoven, since
the latter was no doctor of music, and the former was.
I was led to this digression on account of the difficulty
Handel encountered with his " Te Deum," which could
not be given in any church where the works of doctors
of music only were admitted.   There were five or six
then ; what has become of their names and their work,
and where are they by the side of the name of the immortal " Sassone," who was a genius and no doctor?
It is as Dumas once said to a young gentleman who
was invited to a Russian *soirée*, and was dazzled with
the stars and ribands of the gentlemen present : " Vous
êtes l'homme le plus distingué de la soirée," said Dumas
to him, " vous êtes le seul qui ne soit pas décoré."   And
Frenchmen who are so often ridiculed for this eager
craving after the riband instituted by Napoleon I.,
attach not less value to that distinction than English-
men do to the title of Mus. Doc.

I mentioned King George I. as being angry with
Handel because he preferred the pleasant and luxurious
life at Lord Burlington's, who had received Handel in
his mansion in Piccadilly, to his previous tedious life in
Hanover.   It is interesting to know that Lord Burlington, when asked why he had built his residence *so
far out of town*, where it was " quite a journey for his
friends to visit him," replied, " Well, I like a solitary
life," and he had therefore chosen a site where he was
certain nobody would build near him.   What would he
say to the fields round Piccadilly now ?

We are continually crowing over the great progress
which music has made in this country, and in conse-

quence the heightened position of musicians and the respect with which they are received in society. Handel, who, after having lived with Lord Burlington, was engaged by the Duke of Chandos as conductor of his " chapel," composed there his first oratorio 'Esther,' and the duke was so enchanted with it, that he at once gave Handel, besides his appointment, the sum of a thousand pounds. Has the progress of our days led any duke, however rich, to a similar liberality ?

Handel spoke and wrote several languages, although perhaps not exactly to perfection. In his French correspondence—and French was at that time the language used in the correspondence of distinguished society, just as it is now in Russia—there occur sometimes expressions which might not receive the indulgence of the Académie Française. In a letter to his brother-in-law he promises to give him explanation, " verbally," which he styles *de bouche*, of course a verbal translation of the German *mündlich*. This same letter he signs, " Avec une passion inviolable." Imagine a man to remain his brother-in-law's obedient servant, with " inviolable passion "!

The birthday of Handel and the year of his birth are often incorrectly given, and by whom of all authorities should you think ? By no less a man than Dr. Burney who copied it from Handel's monument in Westminster Abbey, where February 24, 1684, is falsely given, which after minute inquiry and authenticated copy from the church register, has been authoritatively ascertained. The incorrect information coming from such high quarter, it is worth giving here the exact translation of his christening certificate, it being understood that according to the use of those times in Germany the child was christened the day after its birth.

1685.

THE WEEK SAXAGESIMA.

Feb.	*Father.*	*Baptised.*	*Godfathers and Mothers.*	Baptism Register.
* ♀ 24th.	Herr Georg Handel, valet and official surgeon, Camts Chirurgus.	George Frederic.	Herr Philip Fehrsdorff, Saxon intendant at Langendorff, Maid Anna, daughter of G. Taustens, excurate at Giebichstein, and Herr Zacharias Kleinhempel, barber in the market here.	Of the Oberpfarr-kirche (Church of the Holy Virgin), zu Unser Lieben Frauen at Halle anno 1607–1686, p. 663.

This is clear and indisputable evidence. Handel's father, valet and surgeon, was not what we call a surgeon, but according to the German designation, *Bader,* he was a barber of the sort who used to put on leeches, bleed a patient when ordered by the physician, draw teeth, often very badly, and—shave.

Those barbers who even now exist in small German towns and villages proceed from selling leeches to ordering them, and call themselves surgeons, because they meddle with surgical operations of the lowest kind. It

* This sign ♀ means Monday, and shows that Handel was born on Monday 23rd.

is possible that great admirers of Handel imagine that they elevate the man by making him the son of a surgeon. But first of all, the statement is untrue, and what is of more importance in history than truth? And then it seems even more like self-creating genius to have himself only to thank for all he achieved, notwithstanding his low birth.

It is said of Handel that while he enjoyed the hospitality of Lord Burlington he perfected himself not only in the art of composition, but in the art of gastronomy. Indeed the science of eating and more so of drinking was cultivated in those times to such an extent that the Queen is credited with having said that she was herself very proficient in this branch of human science, but that she was compelled to dismiss her faithful Minister, Harley, Earl of Oxford, because he came too often drunk into the Council chamber. Handel had therefore the highest authorities as models from which to copy.

An impartial observer, looking at the publications of the time, will be somewhat startled on finding a score by Handel announced thus : "The Opera of Richard I., for the flute. Ye aires (*sic*) with their symphonies for a single flute, etc. Walsh, 1728. Also may be had where these are sold, all Mr. Handel's Operas for a single flute"!! Another publication was made by Signor Buononcini, who, from jealousy of Handel's overwhelming successes, published, both in English and Italian, a pamphlet, entitled : 'Advice to Composers and performers of Vocal Musick which is *given gratis*, up one pair of stairs in Suffolk Street'; in which he tried to prove that all Handel's vocal compositions were so over-loaded with instrumental accompaniments, that the voice became quite covered, and that instead of being arias they were sonatas.   He did distribute this pamphlet gratis as promised, but is it not remarkable that no number is mentioned—"one pair of stairs in Suffolk Street"?

Rightly to understand why the Italian opera under Handel had at last to give up the ghost, I should require space to show the intrigues, among many other intriguers, of two lady singers, La Faustina and La Cuzzoni.   Those who know what vanity, jealousy, and envy can accomplish among ladies, will understand what the effect of putting both these prima-donnas into the same opera must have been.   But the advent and unprecedented success of the 'Beggars' Opera' put even these ladies in the background, and Polly Peachum (Miss Fenton—Nellie Beswick was her real name) was more adulated, flowered, praised than any of the others. That charming damsel, however, ran away—I should say bolted—with the Duke of Bolton, and everybody thought how very soon she would have to return to her bread-earning profession.   But she was clever enough to become Duchess of Bolton.   The 'Beggars' Opera,' written by Gay and produced by Rich, was such a financial success, that it was said, it made Rich gay, and Gay rich.

Of course Handel got tired of the Italian opera where the ladies above mentioned came to blows on the open stage, where they tore each other's hair, which was all the more unfair as one of the combatants had less to suffer than the other, her hair not growing on her head! Remarkable is a letter written about the "differences" between these two ladies, by the Countess Pembroke to the Mistress of the Robes of Queen Caroline, the Viscountess Sundon.*

In "a letter from a gentleman in town to a friend in the country," London, 1727, the rage of the audience for worn-out Italian reputations in preference to fresh English voices is deplored, and the question is asked whether it is not downright ridiculous that a person should buy from a pawnbroker worn-out secondhand clothes, who can well afford to buy from any shop a fresh new suit?

The world-renowned 'Acis and Galatea' was given in the little theatre in the Haymarket, with the announcement that "tickets may be had and places taken at Mr. Fribourg's, maker of Rappee snuff, at the Play-house gates. Prices 5*s.* and 2*s.* 6*d.*" Handel's glorious oratorio career began with 'Esther,' 1732 (first written in January for the Duke of Chandos).

On July 10th, 1733, 'Athalia' was given in Oxford before 3700 hearers, when before Dr. Arne, M. Charles Floting, and other celebrities, he improvised on the organ so, that they declared such extempore playing had never been heard before on the organ or on any other instrument, and from this moment Handel was considered the greatest man of his time.

---

* The title of the pamphlet relating this notorious affair is: 'The Devil to pay at St. James's, a full and true account of a most horrid and bloody battle between Madame Faustina and Madame Cuzzoni."

I have before said that it was in his advanced years that Handel wrote those oratorios which have since formed a model for students, the admiration of the world, an ever-fresh monument of the activity and fertility of an indefatigable genius, whose works, after one hundred and fifty years, are as fresh and as universally admired as they were when first created. His works must be considered as truly immortal music. I have not the space now to speak of this period of his time, but must leave the consideration of this part of his life and work to another paper. Being one of the most colossal giants of the last century, that century so rich in great men, Handel's life exacts a more than ordinary share of attention, which need not be bestowed on less celebrated men, but to which such a Titan as Handel is fully entitled.

Gluck.

THE discoverer of a new star; the inventor of a new motor-power; the genius that breaks a way through rocks and impediments, supposed to form an impenetrable obstacle for further advance; the navigator who finds a new route, short, to the point, safe; the man, in fact, who lights the torch that dispels the darkness which prevented an ordinary mind from finding an easy way along the stony route which leads to truth; all of these benefactors of humanity share more or less the fate of that man, whom the immense idea struck, to create an instrument for measuring the time and controlling the advance of the sun—otherwise the watch. He was declared mad, and his invention, the " Nüremberg Egg," which he maintained would go on all day and night, with the aid of a very small implement, was deposited in the Rathhaus (Guildhall) as a memento of the deplorable result to which that human folly—called genius, might lead.

Seeing the different fates of different geniuses : how Columbus was at first honoured like a grandee, and allowed the privilege of keeping his hat on in presence of his king, and then thrown into prison, all his immense merits forgotten ; how Mozart, whose work lives

to this day, died so poor that eight shillings paid his
funeral, and debts to the amount of £300 could not be
paid ; whereas Gluck lived in great affluence and luxury,
not because, but although, he too was a genius, the idea
becomes irresistibly clear, that it is not only difficult to
be able to do great things, but that the great acquirement needed is the faculty of making your own success,
of convincing the people of your extraordinary gifts—a
sure help—*though you might not possess them.* What I
mean is, that success in life depends on the *savoir faire* of
a man, because, being given two men of extraordinary gifts
and accomplishments, one does succeed, while the other
one does not, see Gluck and Mozart. And then there
are the mediocrities who have no real desert, but make
a fortune with ordinary house-work, instead of the work-
house to which sometimes more capable men have to go.

Meyerbeer, said to have possessed nine millions of
thalers, never made out of all his operas wherewith to
live comfortably one year. Rossini, who enriched any
amount of publishers and singers with his operas, died
worth three millions, *not* made by music. Dumas, whose
'Mousquetaires' alone made three fortunes, and who was
the author of no less than 1200 volumes, died in debt,
while his contemporary, Victor Hugo, left a princely
income, for, although known to stand as a poet and a
novelist high up the ladder, yet he stood at least equally
high as a maker of bargains with publishers. One of
his greatest achievements before his death was to write
a very small *brochure*, anent the 2nd of December, and
to demand 25,000 francs (£1,000) from his publisher for
it. The publisher refused. What did the great poet

do? He printed it himself; put the price of one franc on it (10*d.*) and sold three hundred thousand copies. Result 300,000 francs or £12,000! This result was due to the simple but eminently practical notion, that there are a vast number of people extant who do not mind spending a shilling, but very spare in comparison are those who can spend half a guinea. And in that one word, "practical," lies the solution of the whole question. Genius creates new works, lives in heaven amid unknown worlds; this is very grand, but practical results are the consequence of common sense on earth. It is not correct to fancy that who can do the bigger, can do the smaller. Man can do the bigger, woman can do the smaller; but that makes man woman's slave, because the ordinary daily requirements, the sewing on of a button, the preparing of your food, the necessary comfort, in fact, has nothing to do with heaven-born genius, but with practical common sense, and therefore has it rightly been said, *Ce que femme veut, Dieu le veut;* and Euripides, when he sent Hercules to Hades to fetch back the shadow of Alceste, which Pluto would not allow, he made Proserpina persuade him to give in, for although Pluto was a god, *Ce que femme veut, Dieu le veut.* All these thoughts come to me as I think over Gluck's career.

Gluck, Christoph Willibald, but not "Ritter von" as he is usually called, for he was neither "Ritter" (knight) nor "von," but merely called himself "Ritter," because he had received a decoration of which he was as the phrase goes Knight "of that order," was born on July 2nd, anno 1714, and simple as this statement seems, it

wanted the inexhaustible patience of research, which is
so often the attribute of German scholars, and in this
instance, that of Mr. A. Schmid, custos of the Imperial
library, Vienna, to fix both date and birthplace. The
place is Weidenwang in Bavaria. Numerous incorrect
biographies give all sorts of Bohemian villages as his
birthplace, alleged to be very authentic, but they are
named simply from rumours or unauthorized assertions,
both lightly made and carelessly repeated. Gluck was
brought to Bohemia when a child, in fact, when three
years old, was taught there, and Bohemia being a very
musical country, and having at various times, even to
this date, produced eminent players and composers, it
was, although not correct, yet not unlikely, that Gluck
should be a Bohemian. Marmontel, who at Gluck's
arrival in Paris, treated him as an intruder, called him
le jongleur de Bohème, but Gluck was a German, and
moreover a Bavarian, for all that. Before venturing upon
giving the reader the chain of facts that form Gluck's
eventful life, ended more than one hundred years ago, I
read a goodly number of English, French and German
sources of information, to which I am indebted for
learning Gluck's history, but to none more than to the
mighty collection of reliable facts—the thoroughly conscientious accumulation and research into every detail
having reference to his hero's life, to be found in
Schmid's 'Life of Gluck,' which can be compared with
one work only, that of another German, Otto Jahn's
'Life of Mozart.' But then you have to take the evil
with the good. First, although reliable in nearly all his
statements, Schmid is too partially smitten with his

idolised hero. Then again you have to wade through an immense series, some hundreds of pages, of certainly undoubted and most patiently verified facts, but they are not always of sufficient importance, and then there are many dreary and tedious observations and annotations, sometimes quite irrelevant, and diluted until barely more than air remains.

Having alluded to his immense success and recognition by all Europe before his death, because his really great masterpieces were only written within the last twenty years of his life, and instantly proclaimed as such (a very unusual luck), I might as well say, that just as he, the prototype of Wagner, broke a new path for himself, and freed his pen from conventional writing, so he set an example to Wagner in the shrewdness of putting himself under the highest patronage and influencing publicity both with his pen and that of his powerful friends. He even sacrificed an excellent French singer (Sophie Arnould), who had very successfully "created" the *rôle* of Eurydice in Gluck's 'Orphée,' for a very pretty girl who, although not without talent, could not compare in artistic inspiration with the other one ; but then, she was the mistress of the Austrian Ambassador, and being himself patronized by the Dauphine, Marie Antoinette, he insured the influence of the court both by legitimate and illegitimate ways.

To begin with, Gluck had the confidence in himself which is granted only to genius. Goethe says somewhere : "Nur Lumpe sind bescheiden" (Only nobodies are modest). Gluck was not arrogant, but he knew his value and he stood up for his system. Not only did he

defend it with a very able pen, but he took all possible
trouble to influence other able pens to take up the
cudgels for him, and so well did they do it, that the
strife soon became general, and, what with praise and
abuse, Gluck's name was perpetually discussed, and his
detractors served as advertisers not a bit less than his
defenders. Again the same proceeding as Wagner's.

What Gluck was anxious to do was this. The Italian
composers made up their mind that the great singers
had the ear of the public, and that in order to please
the public the composer had to please the singers. But
what pleased the singers? An opportunity for special
roulades they could make, or for certain high notes particularly brilliant and which, in order to show well off, they
kept any length of time, whether that destroyed the
harmony of the phrase or not, although this is as big
nonsense as it would be for an actor to hold out a
special vowel in a certain word. But even Gluck, who
preached so wisely against the weakness to flatter the
caprices of a great singer, did he not sacrifice the great
talent of Sophie Arnould to the less talented Saint-
Huberty? He did so, as in other instances many great
men did before and after him, and who, when asked for
their reasons, treated the question as an idle one, because to idle questions you may reply as Martin Luther
did when a lady asked him : " What did the Lord of
creation do during that immensity of time before the
world was created, can you tell me ? "

" I can," said Luther. " He sat in a birch wood, and
cut birches to punish people with, who ask loads of idle
questions."

It is to be feared that Gluck—logical and right in his condemnation of that series of trills and vocalises composed only with a view of furnishing a *cheval de bataille* to a singer, and though he was correct in assigning to music the higher duty of lending expression to deep feeling, to paint in tones dramatic passion, and to impress his hearers with the significance of the poet's words —that he went to the other extreme by appealing to the Greek poets, who had established the principle of unity, which, though grand and life-like, by excluding variety led to monotony. Gluck encountered in his 'Alceste' different despairs of different people anent the same calamity, viz., that occasioned by the gods having decided that King Admetos cannot live unless some one offers himself up as a voluntary victim, when the Queen Alceste decides that she will die for him. Of course this causes her despair at being bound to die so young, and his despair to let her die for him, and the people's despair to let their noble Queen throw away her life. Now it taxes the capabilities of a composer too much to have continually the same feeling to express, though elicited by different persons or reasons, yet always the same tears and cries and wailing. Moreover, this is what people will not sufficiently understand. The Greek nation, great and civilised to a degree in those olden times, with their polytheistic ideas, believed in Apollo and Jupiter, in Pluto and Proserpina, in Charon and Cerberus, in all the gods and semi-gods, in their temples and attributes. But mythology, however poetic and interesting as a study of antiquity, is listened to by us with a smile of cynicism, so that what impressed the

Greeks with deep earnest, and therefore lifted their author Euripides to the highest point of public veneration, cannot possibly impress us in the same serious manner. Gluck feeling this, asked Calsabigi, a talented Italian author, to cut the Greek tragedy into a libretto for him, and he did so.

But I just remember that I should remain more in the regular groove, and instead of speaking at once of the master works which Gluck wrote during the later years of his life, be a good boy and begin from the beginning. Very well, then, let me be a good boy.

It is one of the strange occurrences in the history of art that its ordinary development brings it very slowly forward from step to step, until suddenly a genius springs up and carries all recognised proceedings rapidly away, so that although the plebs may pretend not to understand him, yet real artists cannot withhold their admiration, although it be not impossible that envious professionals may underrate and calumniate him, so that the impression which genius created for a short life-time, and the light which the torch fired by him cast all over the world, may pale again the moment his life flies, and the slow work begin anew. See our nineteenth century now nearly at its conclusion. Gluck one hundred years ago kicked away the sugar-plums of the Italian composers, and created a vigorous dramatic serious element. How long did it last? A very few years after his death the superficial music came again to the fore. Then, behold, from 1810–1830 came that giant Beethoven, and his immense symphonies took the world by surprise. This lasted until in 1850–1860, the supremacy of Offenbach's

opera-buffa sent polkas and valses over the world. Again
came Wagner, with his powerful albeit sometimes tedious
and lengthy creations. So that now, after this long time,
we are again at the music drama as Gluck, a century
before, had thought it. When barely created; it gave rise
to all the violent upholding and tearing down, just as the
Wagner dramas did. It is not right to say : *nil novi sub
sole*—there is nothing new under the sun. New, for us,
is what we have never seen or heard of even, though they
may have had it a thousand years ago. It is clear that
everything on the face of the globe, swinging round in
the same circle, physical and moral history repeats itself.
Pardon the digression. Here is the good boy again.

Gluck was not a wonder-child, as Mozart was. His
father did not produce him, as Mozart *père* did, with
advertisements that " he will play on a piano, when the
keyboard is covered with a cloth, and take no wrong
notes " ; therefore, nobody cried " Au miracle ! " over the
earnest, steady, studious boy, and in general his capacities were developed slowly, and, if I may say so, syste-
matically, not providentially. Mozart had that great
providential inspiration, he sat down to the piano, and
before the public, " phantasied on any given *motif*." I
say providentially, because although every quality of
the mind is given us by Providence, there is yet a great
difference between the work we accomplish through
diligence, industry, and steady development of qualities
born with us, and that heaven-given facility to sit down
and do the astonishing feats that Mozart did when seven
years old, empowered to do so without special trouble
or hard study. Gluck, the son, grandson, and great-

D

grandson of hunters, first inhaled the grand forest air from which he derived the strength that made him vigorous enough in after life unflinchingly to encounter and sustain severe struggles ; for, say what we may, the physical disposition has the principal share in the mind's success. Let any master of painting, of music, of poetry, empty a bottle of brandy, and see what in his dulness he will produce. Let, on the other hand, a strong lad like young Gluck walk out in the early morning hours through a pine wood, and come home filled with ozone, and sit down to work, and his ideas will be strong, healthy, with the wood perfume and the bloom of wild flowers on them, and they will charm every reader. It is this which proves very often the superiority of the English education, because it tends to strengthen and develop the boy's muscles, because in the strong healthy body lodges the strong healthy mind.

The boy Christoph Willibald grew up without much education. He was sent to Komotau to study with the Jesuits in their Gymnasium, but, having no money to pay for his tuition, he discontinued his classes and taught himself singing, fiddle, and violoncello. With the latter instrument, which he played with a certain proficiency, he even made a little money—a most important factor in his impecunious life.

Concerning the Jesuit Gymnasium I have two remarks to offer. Gymnasium in the Austrian states is not what it is here—an institution for developing bodily exercise —but the beginning of a college. A boy, for instance, who wishes to become a lawyer, a doctor of medicine or of theology, must first absolve three years' study of elementary classes, then he is admitted to the gymnasium classes of six years, where at once he begins the study of Latin, Greek, history, and so on. After this come two years' philosophy and physic, and then only is he admitted to the study of medicine, law, or theology, and after three years' theoretical and two years' practical study, to the Rigorosum or final examination, which confers upon him the Doctor's title. At such examinations the professor has a right to ask any question appertaining to the science or sometimes to presence of mind. An intimate friend of your humble servant was asked: "Supposing you would be suddenly fetched to a man who had fallen down from St. Stephen's steeple (ninety-two feet high) on the pavement, what would you do, who would you send for?" "A charwoman," he said, "to sweep away the bones and wash up the blood-stains." And he was praised for his presence of mind, which made him decide, without hesitation, that in such a case reflection was unnecessary, as nothing could be done.

Having explained the gymnasium, I wish to explain the Jesuits. People say that they are the very picture of the self-sacrificing abnegation of the true priest. Any one who knows them, and for the matter of that, other priests in Rome, will judge for himself how far they are entitled to such praise. It always struck me that priests, like every mortal being, live in abstinence when they are so poor that misery is less their choice than their unavoidable fate. When they are rich, cardinals, arch-bishops, or such, you will perhaps see them practise abstinence and abnegation a little more in words than

in fact. So far as I could judge *de visu* a rich cardinal
has the same palace, galaxy of servants, quantity of rich
objets de vertu where virtue is perhaps less object, as
many and as tasteful as Sir Richard Wallace who does not
pose exactly for abstinence. I will say that the Jesuits
whom I have known are the most deeply instructed,
most diplomatically courteous and amiable people one
can wish to meet with. That abnegation is not invariably their guiding principle the instance of young
Gluck may show, who, when he could not pay his fees,
was very simply and unceremoniously told, "Pas d'argent,
pas de Suisse."

I have, as before mentioned, searched rather ob-
stinately for information concerning Gluck's youth, but
strange to say, nothing is known about his second
decennium. Even Schmid, that conscientious searcher,
(so German that he muddled the French word *fuseau*,
fusee or spindle, with *fusil*, rifle,) although he took a life-
time to inquire into every detail having any reference
to the life of his hero, even he seems to have found
no reliable information about Gluck the young man
before he was twenty-four years old, and was introduced
to Count Melzi, who took him as his private secretary to
Italy. Let me say while upon the subject, that Schmid
stated Hercules to be more skilful with the club than
the rifle, the said "rifle" being substituted for the *spindle*,
from which, when playing at the feet of Omphale, he
tried to wind the thread. (Abbé Arnaud, whose French
words in this rather awkward translation are alluded
to, meant to say that effeminate music was not the
affair of the Hercules Gluck, but powerful expression.)

When Gluck arrived in Milan he at once began writing operas after the fashion then established, whereby he at once earned a fashionable reputation. The librettists then wrote for *mise en scène*—that is, opportunities of decorations, costumes, etc.; the composer wrote for voice and "warbling" of solfeggi. Logical dramatic consequences, truth of accent, correct expression adapted to the idea, all that was not thought of much importance. And until Gluck was forty-eight years of age (Mozart was then six), he worked conventionally in the same groove. But suddenly he asked Calsabigi (above referred to) for a Greek libretto, 'Orfeo ed Eurydice,' where, just as in 'Alceste' she enters Hades for her husband, Orpheus goes into the Orcus to fetch back his Eurydice. There, too, although this monotony of hope and despair goes right through the piece, his giant hand cut out of the rock life-size statues, and certainly his scores showed by far more the power of Michael Angelo's Last Judgment than the sweetness of Raphael's Madonna della sedia. Once the new direction entered into, he kept in the same line with his other two 'Iphigénies' and with 'Armida.'

Gluck had at any rate the satisfaction of being recognised as a great celebrity while he was alive, not, as it often happens, a celebrity by name but without the solid gain which only in rare instances rewards those who are clever enough to die before their time, as Rembrandt, the famous Dutch painter, did. He, finding that he had in his studio a great amount, not to say an accumulation, of pictures, sketches, and portraits for sale, left Amsterdam, and told his wife after a certain time, to give out the

news of his having suddenly died.   Barely had the news
got abroad than friends and art patrons and dealers
flocked to the house of the disconsolate widow, offering
sympathy, and proving anxious to acquire whatever they
could get of the great man's work.   Each wishing to buy,
one overbid the other, and whatever was to be had, was
bought most eagerly.   Barely had a month passed, when
Rembrandt quietly returned to Amsterdam, and far
from being cross, the people laughed at the clever trick.
Again we might say, Do not complain of that, there is
nothing new under the sun.   We are such infinitely
small points on one of the smallest globes in creation,
that so far as our own history goes, men were always
governed by the same wishes, the same wants, and more
or less by the same capacities.   In every century one or
two extraordinary organizations in art, deserving the title
of genius, suddenly appear struggling for contemporary
appreciation, yet are they thoroughly understood only half
a century later, and this process continually renews itself.
Just as in the general darkness God said, " Let there be
light," so in the general darkness of ordinary course and
mediocrity the genius comes like a sunlight and throws
its bright rays on art and science, and that goes on for
a certain time, then reaction follows, and when the new
century is at an end, again another torch is lighted and
goes through the same proceeding.   The globe is round,
all movement is round, and the quicker you rush on
from one point of departure the quicker you must come
back to it by completing your circular movement.   The
padre Martini, himself an Italian, deploring the routine
into which music had fallen in France by the end of the

last century, felt and foresaw the necessity of a genius coming and reforming the meaningless conventionality, and this is what he wrote: "È desirabile che rinasca qualche professore di raro talento, e ben istruito di tutte le parti della musica, il quale, senza curarsi dei propositi impertinenti di tutti i suoi rivali, faccia risorgere all' esempio dei Greci, l'arte di muovere le passioni e libera finalmente gli ascoltanti dal tedio che loro fa provare la musica dei giorni nostri," (Martini's 'Storia della musica.') (It would be desirable that there be born a professor of rare talent and well versed in all the scientific parts of music, who, without caring a bit about the impertinent remarks of his rivals, would revive that great art of the Greeks to excite the real passions, and deliver the audiences from that tedious bore which the music of the present day causes them to put up with.)

When Gluck composed his 'Armida,' the critics said that it was not to be believed that his verses were the same that Lulli had set to music, because Lulli had made them a mere peg whereon to hang his musical hobbies, whereas Gluck was so penetrated with the meaning of the words, that on that occasion he made his celebrated speech: "When I write an opera, I try before all to forget that I am a musician," which has been so thoroughly misunderstood. What he meant to say was, that he entered so entirely heart and soul into the subject which he had to interpret musically, that he identified himself with the poet more than with the musician.

The opinion of German critics on Gluck is naturally

very favourable; but such men as Berlioz, in France, and Schuré, in Belgium, wrote in an equally inspired strain on him. Berlioz says: "The exceptional qualities of Gluck will perhaps never again be found combined in the same musician. Inspiration, which carries the audience with him, high logic, a grand style, abundant ideas, deep knowledge of dramatising his orchestra, catching melody, always correct expression, both natural and picturesque, a seeming disorder which in fact is only a more high class order, clearness of design, and above all, power of such immensity that it had sometimes a frightening effect on an imagination capable of appreciating him."

To understand the difficulty of performing Gluck, and hence to understand him, unless interpreted to perfection, you need only read what he himself says about the famous air of Orpheus: 'J'ai perdu mon Eurydice': "Change the slightest *nuance* of movement or accent, and you'll make a dance tune of it." Now, as that air is one that has to be sung first with despair, then with tears in the voice, it is self-evident that only such artists who take the trouble thoroughly to understand the intentions of the composer can hope successfully to undertake the interpretation of his works. One reason, perhaps, why these operas produced such effect on the audiences of those times was, that they were given in moderate-sized theatres, calculated for the natural proportions of acoustics. Concert halls, like the Albert Hall, calculated to be filled by exceptional organs only, are no use when those exceptional organs are not available; and we have, moreover, gone up always higher in pitch, because the instruments sound more brilliantly in higher positions, and have built theatres and halls in which shouting becomes an unavoidable condition. Shouting, however, is not art; and for building these big halls there is only one *motif:* making money, by admitting numbers of people at cheap prices, who cannot see or even conveniently hear. But that is not art, and the whole process of making music in this fashion is much more commercial than artistic.

When Gluck, after the great success of ' Orfeo,' gave ' Alceste,' the people failed at first to take in the grandeur of the new work, and received it on the first evening rather coldly. Gluck, in despair, met Arnaud after the performance, and said to him : " Oh, mon ami, 'Alceste' est tombée." " Oui, tombée du ciel," said Arnaud. " Only give them time to elevate themselves to that height." This shows what devoted friends Gluck had in Paris. And how intolerant towards others those admirers sometimes became (just like Wagnerites), the following little anecdote will demonstrate.

Dorat, another admirer of Gluck, stood, one evening, in the pit, among a number of friends of the great composer, when some unknown listener asked him what he thought of Gluck. " Gluck," said Dorat, " is a musician of the first water, probably the first for grand effects, powerful, passionate, as warm as energetic, and who rends your soul with a shout of despair. He is elevated even in his orchestral accompaniments ; it is he who blew life into your automatic chorus by the power of his genius : in one word, he is the man to create the long-needed revolution in music. I find, though, that he is in some exceptional moments rather strepitous at the expense of melody." "Oh, you are a Piccinist?" "I never saw the man, and know not a note of his music." "Never mind, you see a fault in Gluck : you are a Piccinist!" So it happened to the writer of these lines to be asked during an opera night in Covent Garden Theatre, why he had quarrelled with Madame Patti. "But who says that I have quarrelled with her?" "Oh, you have praised Madame Nilsson ; that is evidently proof enough that you quarrelled with Madame Patti!"

I mentioned that Gluck dedicated his 'Alceste' to the Grand Duke of Tuscany, and in his dedication-preface developed all that he thought of conventionality and thoughtless abuse of music, the real strength of which he only saw in lending to the poet's thought additional power, and in lending picturesque expression to the ideas of the drama, instead of hooking any amount of trills and runs on the peg of the verses, which might express anything between a murder and a bill of fare. And who, you may ask, was the Duke of Tuscany? It was he who became the enlightened Emperor Joseph II. of Austria, who, a hundred years ago, foresaw the triumph of liberty over the dark principles of feudalism ; he who abolished all that contributed to the suppression of freedom, who sapped at the root of what Gambetta called, *L'Ennemi,* abolished monasteries, confessional, the exaggerated number of holidays; it was he whose statue was crowned with laurels and flowers on the 15th of March, 1848, when Austria broke her fetters and enforced a constitution. To him Gluck inscribed his opera and the preface, in which he maintained that he freed opera from the worst of tyrants, "inveterate bad habit."

Marie Antoinette, proud to patronize her countryman and previous teacher, wrote to Marie Christine: "A glorious triumph at last with Gluck's 'Iphigénie.' The audience, though, seemed at first puzzled with the new system, but now the excitement is such in society that people quarrel and fight over it as if a religious question were at stake." Gluck told Marie Antoinette that the air of France had redoubled the power of his genius, and that the sight of her majestic beauty had given such impetus to his ideas, that like herself, they had become sublime and angelic. "And when," asked she, "shall we hear 'Armida'?" "C'est sur le point d'être fini, et vraiment cela sera superbe!" said Gluck. With the same modesty, Spontini, at the moment of beginning the dress rehearsal of his opera, 'La Vestale,' said: "Messieurs, l'opéra que vous allez entendre est un chef-d'œuvre, commençons!" Vestris, the well-known ballet-master, not being afforded sufficient display for his dances, told Gluck, "If you persist in your refusal, the success of 'Armida' is sure to be doubtful." (The same thing was told Wagner, twenty-five years ago, when he was on the point of bringing out 'Tannhäuser' in Paris, and refused to write ballet music for it.) "My subject," said Gluck, "is taken from the 'Gierusalemme liberata.' There is consequently not much room for *entrechats*. If Torquato Tasso had wished to make Rinaldo a dancer, he would not have brought him out in the armour of a warrior."

Dr. Burney in his journal of a musical tour, 1773, speaks about his visit to Gluck in the Faubourg St. Marc, where he had very elegant well-furnished rooms. " Gluck," he says (then nearly sixty), "was much pitted with the small-pox and very coarse in figure and in look, but was very soon put into the best of humours by accompanying his niece, then a girl of thirteen, upon a very bad harpsichord, several airs of ' Alceste.' She had a very powerful voice, infinite expression and an astounding execution, considering that she was taught only two years. Gluck himself sang from ' Iphigénie,' of which he had not yet committed one note to paper, which shows that he carried the work in his head nearly ready. (This is also the explanation of Mozart writing the overture to 'Don Juan' in a few night hours, because he carried it written as it were in his mind.) He played with a readiness as if he had the full score before him, which astonished me much." The real origin of the Piccini and Gluck struggle was that Louis XV. and Madame Dubarry had always patronized Italian music, and when the latter saw that Marie Antoinette took up Gluck, she felt doubly incited to oppose to her influence her own *protégé* Piccini who was a Neapolitan.

The *Journal de Paris* of the 21st January, 1777, tells the following story. During the performance of 'Alceste' "tragédie de Mons. W. A. Gluck," Mdlle. Levasseur sang the verse : " Il me déchire et m'arrache le cœur" with such deep expression that a gentleman in the stalls felt perfectly enchanted with her and applauded with frenzy. A neighbour of his, however, of quite different opinion, shouted to the singer : "It is not the heart, it is my ears you tear off;" whereupon the first gentleman got up and said : "What a lucky accident for you ; now go quickly and try and get another pair." And of course everybody laughed and applauded the singer. It has often been said that Frenchmen cannot resist ridicule, but who can ? If as the wise old king, Solomon, said : "All is vanity," being laughed at must be the severest trial.

Gluck had this great problem to solve : "Truth in art." So long as there have existed æsthetical and philosophical discussions on art this question has always been debated. In order to be true in art, must you represent, or are you allowed to represent what may be horrid in nature ? Lessing put down the rule once for all : What is not handsome, forms not a fit subject for artistic treatment (Was nicht schön ist, gehört nicht in die Kunst), and although really true representation and expression are most desirable in a work of art, there is certainly no necessity for choosing a subject the truth of which would only give most unpleasant impressions.

Gluck knew well what he was about, and, as I said before, he knew how to use his pen. One of his great adversaries, La Harpe, who understood nothing about music, having violently attacked 'Alceste,' Gluck wrote to him : " I am extremely sorry to have been misled by the number of performances and the applause granted to my operas into the belief that the public liked them. I am happy to see that it is sufficient to be a man of letters to judge everything, and I perceive with admiration that you have learned more about music in a few hours than

I who practise it over forty years.   Since from what you
say it is clear that a singer ought to continue the same
motive, when he passes from one impression, even from
one passion into another, I shall take advantage, knowing your predilection for tender airs, to make Achilles,
however furious he may be, sing an air of such sweetness that everybody will cry, and I shall omit every
instrument from the orchestra except the oboes, flutes,
and violins, so that no noise shall disgrace your tender
nerves, and nothing be heard but what is soft and sweet.
Perhaps some one will object that Sophocles made
Oedipos appear with eyes injected with blood, furious
with passion, terrible to behold, but then I shall reply to
this connoisseur, that Mons. de la Harpe prefers that in
his most furious anger, music serve only to express the
sounds of turtle-doves.   Some of my friends went even
so far as to tell me to go and study your works, and try
to find out whatever mistakes there may be discovered.
' But,' said I, ' I am a musician, and dare not bear an
impious hand on so great a writer's work.'   ' Why,' said
they, ' has not M. de la Harpe, who is a literary man,
without the slightest scruple tried to demolish the work
of a musician, which, he says himself he understands
nothing about, and moreover proves what he says by
the expressions he used when exposing his opinion.'
You see, my dear sir, if I told a painter to combine the
sweetness of colours and delicacy of design with the
coquettish grace of a flirting woman, when drawing the
Last Judgment, he might answer me : I should like
nothing better, but he might add the words of Apelles
to Alexander—' Don't talk so loud, for the little boy

there who crushes the colours for me might hear you
and mock at your words.' "

This shows that he was well able to defend himself,
but gleaning among the fiery sparks which the heated
discussion elicited, one finds such phrases as, " Il y a de
très belles choses dans les opéras italiens, mais les
Italiens n'ont pas encore produit un opéra qui soit une
belle chose," which proves what at first sight seems a
paradox, that you express a higher opinion of a work
when you remark that it contains feeble points than
when you say that there are some good points in it ;
because, in the first case, the beautiful is the rule, though
there be weak points ; in the second case it is the reverse.

When Gluck complained to Dorat, that he received
so many stupid letters anent his operas, whether admiring or criticising them, Dorat said, " L'enthousiasme ou
la haine des sots, sont les deux malheurs du génie," and
those who are uncharitably enough disposed to admit
that " les sots " form the majority of mankind, may feel
nearly inclined to pity genius. So is this remark of
special interest when we compare it with what is continually said about the sonority of contemporaneous
music : " Power is the work of genius ; whoever tries to
imitate it creates only noise." A child which screams
will never be heard like a man with a powerful organ,
however calmly he may speak.

Gluck had that unfailing, unwavering judgment to
know what he had to do. He swept away the superficial series of fioritures and gave his music a firmness of
character which people did not always at first conceive.

When he wrote 'Artaserse,' some musicians blamed him for his new track. So he thought he would have his fun with them, and he wrote a great air, but only one, entirely in the style of the old claptrap with a vengeance, and he had the immense satisfaction to see by the side of the success of his real music, that very air hissed to such an extent that it had to be cut out of the score. Calm and thoughtful in his work, he was yet very hasty and hot tempered in ordinary life, and it happened to him sometimes to receive fierce lessons. For instance, having lost his temper once with his servant, he suddenly shouted to him : " This is really unbearable, are you mad, or am I ? " " Oh," humbly replied the man, " surely your Excellency would not keep a servant who is mad ? " The reason of the row was a very funny one. Gluck had a housekeeper who was a great miser, and in order to find out whether the servant took occasionally a piece of sugar, she had recourse to the following stratagem. She tried patiently to catch a fly. When she succeeded, she put it quickly in the sugar-bowl, and put the cover on. From time to time she looked to see was the fly still there. Of course when she found the prisoner had gone, she knew that somebody must have delivered him. Then she pounced upon the servant as the guilty party. But as it happened, Gluck had perpetrated the crime, hence the reproach of the servant who was innocently accused.

Gluck wrote in 1741 'Artaserse,' in 1742 'Demofonte,' 1743 'Siface,' and 1744, 'Fedra,' two operas for Venice ; what with Milan, Turin, and Venice, he wrote eight operas in five years. Lord Middlesex, then theatrical manager of the Haymarket, London, engaged him as composer, and he travelled with his great patron, Prince F. P. Lobkowitz, *viâ* Paris to London. But when he arrived (in 1745) the theatre was closed, on account of the public prejudice against all the singers being Catholics. Performances began again on the 7th of January, 1746, with his new opera, 'La Caduta dei Giganti,' given in presence of the Duke of Cambridge to whom the opera was dedicated. The opera had but a moderate success, in consequence of which only five performances were given. But Dr. Burney's fine perception guessed the genius, and he wrote anent the opera that "it was evident, notwithstanding the quiet appreciation of the work by the public, that from that young man great things were to be expected." Gluck wrote to Handel about it, to ask the great man's advice, and he replied to Gluck : "You have been too conscientious ; you have taken too much trouble with your work ; that does no good here. The English people want something striking, that touches directly their eardrum." Gluck differing in this from many people, that having asked for advice he acted upon it, instantly added two trombones to the score, and—the success increased. I wonder whether Handel meant that Gluck took too much trouble with details, because that is literally the advice I once heard Rossini give to a young composer : "Take trouble only with the great pieces ; don't waste your attention and your time on small matters ; put down the columns and the pillars, never mind the petty woodwork." When Gluck was in England he had not yet reached that great epoch of self-confidence which

E

made him finally throw over with a mighty hand all
the conventionalities, but he took advantage of the
advice of Handel and Dr. Arne (1710–1778), and had
part of his opera 'Artaserse' here published. The
exact title was, 'The favourite songs in ye Opera called
Artaserse. By Sig. Gluck, London. Printed for J. Walsh
in Catharine Street in ye Strand.'

From this time dates Gluck's turning-point, when he
made up his mind to leave sweet music for grand music.
Sweet music goes straight to your ear, and tickles it,
and pleases it, as sweets may please your palate. Grand
music impresses your mind, it goes to your brain and to
your heart, and is solid food, substantial tonic, not mere
sugar-plums. How deeply inspired, however, the young
composer was, there came a moment when the *man*
claimed his right. He fell in love with the attractive
daughter of the banker, Pergin — Marianne was her
name. The mother sided with him and her daughter,
but the father, a purse-proud man, would not hear of the
marriage with a man of " hopes." But after travelling
to Rome, where he wrote for the Teatro Argentina his
'Telemaco,' he was informed of the death of old Pergin
and quickly returning, he got married on the 15th of
September, 1750, being then thirty-six years of age, and
not for one moment to his life's end did the mutual love
of the two slacken. Remarkable is the circumstance
that he was commissioned in 1761 to write a ballet,
'Don Juan,' which is entirely composed on the very
subject which has served Mozart to write his opera from.
His first real revelation came in 1762, when Gluck refused Metastasio's sweet opportunities for music which he

found not dramatic enough, and told Calsabigi to write him a great libretto with real passions, and importance enough for a tone drama (*vide* Wagner), for which he asked him to take Orfeo and Euridice. He begged of Metastasio, who was not in favour of the new departure, not to oppose it in public, and let him have a chance, which Metastasio promised. The first impression on the public was intense astonishment. The musicians were deeply impressed at once ; and when the opera was given for the fifth time, it was understood by all, and the effect upon the public by the grand inspiration of the Greek poet so skilfully used by Calsabigi, the strange power of the music, and the dramatic performance, Gluck having insisted on making even the chorus act for the first time in their career, produced a profound effect.

On the 2nd of January, 1765, Josef II. was married to Princess Maria Josepha of Bavaria. For this solemnity Gluck had the honour of composing ' Il Parnasso confuso,' which on the 23rd of the same month was sung by four Archduchesses, Maria Elisabetta, Maria Amalia, Maria Josepha, and Maria Carolina, all excellent sopranos, as Maria Theresa herself had been. Gluck made Calsabigi again take his subjects from Euripides, because his own maxim was that of the Greeks : Unity and truth ! He made him change Euripides' scenario of Alceste, inasmuch as in the original Euripides makes Hercules intervene when Alceste is in the power of the Tartarus, and by sheer force tear her away, whereas Calsabigi makes Apollo the mediator, who having received Admetos' hospitality, intercedes in Alceste's favour. I just mention this because so much erroneous

stuff has been written about Euripides and Calsabigi, as
if Greek and Italian were beyond the reach of mankind
and belonging, like the mammoth bones, to an ante-
diluvian period.

It must interest English readers to learn what one of
the quoted names, regarded as a universal authority,
thought of Gluck and his work. I have before alluded
to Dr. Burney, who in his diary (two volumes) mentions
the desire he had when in Vienna to make Gluck's
acquaintance. So he asked Viscount Stormont, then
English Ambassador at Vienna, to arrange an appointment with Countess Thun, whose great desire it was to
bring the two great men together, and so they two, with
Dr. Burney, repaired to the Rennweg where Gluck lived.
The meeting seems to have been a very cordial one.
Gluck, though at the time fifty-eight years old, sang himself, and Dr. Burney says that although completely voice-
less, the expression and grace of his declamation made
a profound impression upon him. But the real musical
wonder in the house was Gluck's niece, already mentioned, the daughter of his sister. The girl was then
thirteen years old, but it seems that her voice, her
dramatic passion, and the peculiarly vibrating power of
her organ moved the hearer deeply. Unfortunately, the
poor girl died at the age of sixteen from the smallpox.
Dr. Burney says of Gluck's composition literally this :
" As to invention, especially dramatic painting and
theatrical effect, neither living nor dead composer equals
him. He studies for a long time his libretto, carefully
weighs the single parts, and the foundation of every
character. It is his endeavour to satisfy the mind and

the feeling of his audience. He is not only the friend
of the poet—he becomes the poet himself. In the vocal
part he exhibits a study of nature and simplicity, and
his orchestral accompaniments are a rich palette, and
thus he is a painter too." Gluck found that the English public loved simplicity, and therefore he adopted
this manner, and he told Dr. Burney that he owed to
England his predilection for the simple and impressive
style which had so singularly distinguished his operas
from the Italian flimsiness of his time.

As to Gluck's singing without voice but so impressive
through its passion, Dorat, one of the great poets of the
time, when told that such a toneless voice sounded
rather false, said :—

> " Il échappe souvent des sons à la douleur,
>   Qui sont faux pour l'oreille, mais vrais pour le cœur."

Of the numerous extremely spirituels words which
the enthusiasm for and against the music of Gluck
elicited, I will quote only a few—although volumes have
been written—of the most interesting kind. Thus wrote
Voltaire to an antagonist of Gluck—the Marquise du
Deffau—with hypocritical deference, on the 25th of
January, 1775 : " I ask your generous pardon, madame,
for admiring Gluck, or rather the Chevalier Gluck. I
thought I had told you that a lady of great beauty with
an excellent voice, which is quite equal to that of
Mdlle. Le Maure, sang to me a récitatif-mesure by this
reformer, and gave me infinite pleasure. Although I
am as deaf as blind when the snow silvers the Alps and
the Mount Jura, I really beg your pardon for having so

enjoyed Gluck's work. Possibly I was wrong. It is quite true that other works of the same maëstro are much less beautiful. I feel nevertheless that this is the music which, with the little sympathy I conceive for mere matters of fancy and taste, affects me most thoroughly, and for all that, like you, Madame la Marquise, I love the work of Lully notwithstanding all the Glucks of creation."

This is what Abbé Arnaud wrote in answer to Marmontel, who attacked Gluck by principle :

> " Marmontel juge la peinture en aveugle,
> Et la musique comme un sourd,
> Il dit qu'il a le secret des vers de Racine,
> Jamais secret ne fut si bien gardé."

Gluck, through his excellent wife accustomed to great neatness and cleanliness, cared very much for his appearance, and, according to the fashion of the times, was often seen in an embroidered costume, and wearing a cane with a gold knob. His death was quite sudden. He drove out with his wife, and in the carriage an apoplectic stroke rendered immediate return to his house necessary. He was put to bed. His friends tried to deceive him about the danger his life was threatened with, and began a discussion about a sacred trio he had written, and very much disputed the tone in which the part of the Saviour should be sung. "Well, my friends," he said, " as you cannot decide how we can make the Saviour sing, I'll go to Him and ascertain from His holy countenance what to do," and he died placidly on Nov. 15, in the year 1787.

I mentioned that the row which was made by the

adversaries of Gluck in Paris was advertised under the flag of Piccinists and Gluckists, but not only had the two composers no share in the animosity, but the *Journal de Paris,* of December 13th, in the year 1787, published one of the most touching, noble-minded letters, written by Piccini, proposing the institution of an annual concert at the Opera, with nothing but Gluck's music, and an anniversary regularly established with one of Gluck's operas—Signor Piccini himself to conduct the first evening. Madame de Genlis in her 'Souvenirs' especially mentions the circumstance that Gluck always spoke well of Piccini. It is therefore quite out of place to charge the two composers with the gossips of those low-minded persons who imagine that they cannot better serve the interest of an artist than by lowering any other man supposed to be his rival.

There is an amount of poetry committed to Gluck's memory, which, with the exception of a dozen Spanish lines by Yriarte, breathing real poetry and warm feeling, is perfectly horrible. French and German and Italian was the galimathias unlimited, but one Bridi carries off the palm with a Latin epitaphium sufficient to revolt the spirit of the great composer in his grave.

Gluck was, like many a genius, too far in advance of his time to be immediately appreciated to his full value, but he had the common sense to live long enough to insure a great share of his due, and he had tact, cleverness, and flexibility sufficient to make friends of those whose influence could help him in some way or other. He has been reproached with having too much courted

contemporaneous celebrities, but when you see a man
like Jean Jacques Rousseau, after having decidedly given
up going to the Opera, making it his business to be seen
every time a Gluck opera was performed, when a man of
the immense importance of Voltaire takes up his pen
to write such a letter as above quoted, the great impression which the testimony of such men creates upon the
general public is well worth a few letters, as Henry IV.
said : " Paris vaut bien une messe."

While in art always the great reformer, the bold inno-
vator of his time, Gluck, in private life, having married
for love, remained faithful to the wife he had chosen,
and who was the most touchingly faithful companion to
him until the very moment of his death.   In domestic life
as well as in his creations, he was a model to be respected
and admired, and worthy, if possible—of being imitated.

Abrupt, dictatorial haughtiness was not in Gluck's
character, but he was none the less convinced that he
was justified in entering new paths which he had the
strength to enforce, and however velvety was the paw
that held the pen when he wrote the dedication of his
'Alceste' to the Duke of Braganza, he made it well
understood that he was determined to do away with the
abuses and illogical habits of the Italians who wrote arias
only as show-pieces, and that he boldly put in the place
of the discarded flimsiness his well thought out dramatic
plan, because he knew it to be superior to the base con-
cessions which Italian composers weakly conceded to
the vanity of celebrated singers.

A long chapter might be written on the tyranny of
singing celebrities and on the submission of great

composers ; but that will always be so, and, to judge
from recent experience, will grow worse. A singer, who
twenty years ago received two hundred pounds for a
season of three months, receives now seven or eight
hundred pounds for one evening, and it is an open secret
that the very same singer is about beginning an operatic
tour in North America where the payment of that *prima
donna* exceeds a thousand pounds of our money per
evening. How dare a composer resist the wishes of
such a singer ?

A Chevalier de Castellux, an ignoramus A1, pretended
to discuss the merits of Gluck and Piccini with the
Marquis de Clermont, a great friend and admirer of
Gluck's Muse, but the latter replied, " I will sing you an
air, and if you are capable of beating correct time to it,
I will discuss Gluck with you." This may seem rather
severe, but it is well-nigh incredible to what an extent
ignorance and arrogance assume a right of discussion.
It has happened to the writer of these lines to be present
when a gentleman violently attacked Thalberg's piano
playing as compared with that of Liszt. And in the
course of conversation it was elicited that the gentleman
in question had never heard either Liszt or Thalberg !

It is a well-known fact that Gluck wrote his best
operas after he was sixty years old, so that the last
years of his life saw his most glorious works. If Rossini
had not stopped writing after producing ' William Tell,'
when he was thirty-seven years old, what masterpieces
might he have given to the world ! But he would not
be persuaded into leaving his adored idleness. Count
Aguado, the distinguished Spanish banker and amateur,

a short time after the success of 'William Tell,' wrote to
Rossini, who then lived in Bologna, would he send him a
new work, or would he allow the Count to send him a
libretto, Rossini to fill out a blank cheque, which Count
Aguado would be happy to send him the moment his
score was written.   For two weeks no answer came, but
then a letter arrived marked "Immediate," in which
Rossini announced a parcel to be on its way to Paris,
which the count fully expected to be the longed-for
score.   Great was his surprise when he read the following lines : " Monsieur le Comte, I have the honour
to announce to you that by this day's post I have forwarded to your address in Paris a parcel containing what
cost me much reflection and care, a mortadella of the
finest description, together with one of the best
Bolognese sausages.   There is only just a soupçon of
garlic in it, and I hope you will find it to your taste, and
remember your ever devoted friend, Gioachino Rossini."
Of the demanded score not one single word neither then
nor ever afterwards.

The great friendship which the famous Salieri had for
Gluck was expressed in a very amusing manner, a poly-
glot leave-taking so often resorted to by Italians, who
know just a little of every language, when Gluck left for
Paris, and Salieri addressed him thus : " Ainsi, mon cher
ami, lei parte domani per Parigi. Je vous souhaite di cuore
un bon voyage.   Sie gehen in eine Stadt wo man die
fremden Künstler schätzt, e lei ci farà onore, ich zweifle
nicht (embracing him).   Ci scriva, mais bien souvent ! "
And he did them "onore," because Gluck lived and died
one of the greatest stars on the musical horizon.

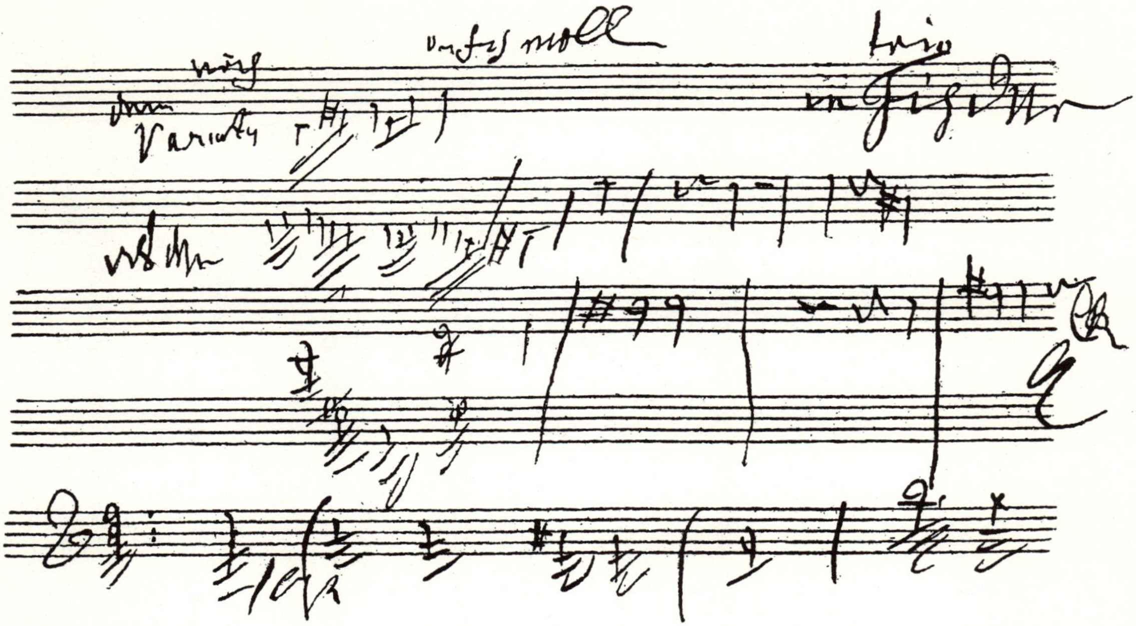

FACSIMILE OF A MS. SKETCH BY BEETHOVEN.

Beethoven.

WHOEVER wishes to know the real musical giant of the nineteenth century, the overwhelmingly great genius of modern times, in fact the man whom we may safely call the father of the great orchestral work created in this century, the very foundation stone upon which all modern master-works are built, will receive from every honest musician the answer : Ludwig van Beethoven. Although his life has been described most minutely and most ably by biographers of many nations, by intimate personal friends who for years had noted down every particular, every little anecdote, every word worth preserving ; although these more faithful than brilliant writers— more voluminous than luminous, as Sheridan says— have been followed by writers much better able to appreciate the great man and his work from a safer distance, so that there is no hope of communicating anything new with regard to facts or opinions; yet I venture to offer a few remarks on this Colossus of Composition : first, because I should be sorry to have such a name missing in a Gallery of Composers on whom it was my good fate to write a small series of essays ; and also because I fancy that the numerous books of reference from which information on the subject may be gathered are for the most part less accessible to the general public, being either exclusively musical or published in foreign languages, each nation being, as it were, jealous to contribute a small share to the glorious monument of him who excited the admiration of every country—one might say of every man and woman—taking an interest in music.

As seven towns fought for the honour of being the birthplace of Homer, so are there several houses in several streets of the good City of Bonn on the Rhine which not only claim the honour of having been the birthplace of Beethoven, but there are actually two houses provided with memorial tablets, both stating that "in this house Beethoven was born." Hoping to learn the real truth with my own eyes, I thought it as well to take a little trouble and make a journey to Bonn, to see his monument and investigate the affair on the spot.

Bonn is situated on the border of the Rhine, just where that river is most charming ; and although the part of the journey from Mayence to Coblentz may not justify its high reputation, the spot from Coblentz to Cologne certainly does ; and nobody would guess from the poetical, romantic outside of Bonn, how dirty and unpoetical is the inside, how the streets smell, how the houses are kept, and even in what an uninviting state is the Beethoven monument itself, which ought to be one of the attractions of the town, and an ornament, artistic and historical. I had no idea, when I arrived at the splendid railway station, that the whole place surrounding the monument would not be penetrated by that reverential air that usually fills places where marble reminiscences of great men form the pride of a town when it comes in for an honor which it has done nothing to deserve. The least anybody might expect, surely, is that the monument of so great a man, in a city which otherwise has little to boast of, might be kept decently clean. But even this modest expectation is doomed to disappointment. Imagine a dirty Square with the statue in the middle, two lanterns equally dirty, so that even the light of Beethoven's genius could not shine through them ; the statue adorned (?) with a thoroughly decayed laurel crown, boasting two equally dirty white (?) ribands, on which the name St. Cecilia appears, either as a concession to the society who offered this petty homage, or as an invocation to the patron saint of music to save from the surrounding dirt the genius whose purity in art was equalled by his purity of character in life. The only thing grand and indestructible in the affair is the great name and the absence of superfluous eulogy. One must be thankful for small mercies ; and that the name BEETHOVEN has been allowed to stand there alone, grand in its simple glory, without any of those usual sentimental German poesies, is a blessing indeed.

My pilgrimage to the house began with a walk to the Bonngasse 20, where a tablet erected by the town attracts the curious traveller. On the tablet are engraved in German the words, " In this house Ludwig van Beethoven was born, on the 17th December in the year 1770." The house is kept by a Restaurant called Blech, which, considering that Beethoven especially gave effect to the brass in the orchestra ("Blech," means brass in German), may be considered ominous. The house certainly looks by no means imposing, but the

misery of the interior is even more depressing than one
would expect from the outside.   Imagine a bad wooden
staircase leading up to the first floor, and hence a wind-
ing, shockingly narrow second floor stair which brings
you up to a garret-room some ten feet by six, containing
a bed and a chest of drawers said to have belonged to
the furniture then in the room.   There is a large hole in
the floor, which Mrs. Blech, who acted as my kind cice-
rone, told me could not be repaired, as it was necessary
to keep the room in its ancient hysterical state.   She
said " hysterisch," but I take it " historisch" is what she
meant.   The same kind lady informed me that Beethoven's father was a conductor (*Kapellmeister*), " but
then," she added apologetically, as if to excuse the humble
station, " he was a tailor as well ! "   She has lived there
fifteen years, and seems to make an honest penny out of
foreigners coming to see the humble cradle of the great
man ; and she told me that she continues the tradition
by giving Concerts in winter down in the yard while
people sit at the table drinking beer or lager.   I don't
know whether these Concerts include the ' Eroica ' or
the ' Pastoral,' though the latter would more probably
suit the character of the audience.   Of course she is
most indignant when anybody mentions the other house
as being the birthplace of Beethoven.   " On *this* house,"
she explains, " the town has erected the tablet, and this
is the true one ; on the other the landlord himself put it
up, but Beethoven was over five years old when they
came to live there, and, great as the man was, he cannot
have been born five years old, can he, now ? "   Most
certainly I was of her opinion ; yet, in order to judge *de*

visu, I repaired to the Rhinegasse No. 7, a much better looking house; but the street is horrid—quite near the Rhine, though, where the necessary element for cleansing could easily be procured; and I found it true that the tablet, with the suspiciously short inscription "Beethoven's Geburtshaus," has been put up by the present proprietor. The street, narrow and very unevenly paved, is not exactly in the odour of sanctity, for which fact, I fervently hope, the several sausage-makers and pork-pie manufacturers there established may one day have to answer.

There is a certain difficulty about fixing the day of Beethoven's birth; the only thing known is the day when he was baptized; and, as it was usual to baptize the child the day after its birth, the 17th of December is accepted as his birthday, but not with certainty, because when poor people could not make it convenient to go on a certain day, they waited a day or two; and among the numerous volumes which I have consulted, there is one in which the 16th is positively given as the date. The house where he was born, and which I have stated to be situated in the Bonngasse 20, is sometimes mentioned as 515, the old number from the time when the houses of the whole town were numbered from 1 to 1000; not as now, where there are only as many numbers as there are houses in a street. Frau Baum, who is a neighbour, still gives her number as 516. The year is undoubtedly 1770, not 1772, as Beethoven seemed to believe himself, and which must be incorrect, from the simple circumstance that he so well remembered his grandfather, who died in 1773, when Beethoven was

three years old ; whereas if his account were correct
he would have been only a baby of barely one year.
As to the several houses where he lived as a child,
it is established beyond doubt that he was born in
the Bonngasse, whence the family went to the Dreieck
(triangle), and then to the Rhinegasse, when Ludwig was
five years old.   I will now give the baptismal register,
whereby hangs a tale.   It runs thus : " *Département de
Rhin et Moselle : Mairie de Bonn.   Extrait du Registre
des naissances de la paroisse de St. Remy à Bonn.*   Anno
millesimo septingentesimo, die decima septima Decem-
bris, baptizatus est Ludovicus.   Parentes D. Joannes
van Beethoven et Helena (vel Magdalena) Keverich,
conjuges.   Patrini D. Ludovicus van Beethoven et Ger-
trude Müller, dicta Bannes."

This copy of the original document is marked " Pour
extrait conforme, 2 Juin 1810."   Signature and seal.
When it was examined, an objection was raised that
this could not be correct ; and in fact the objection was
not long ago repeated, viz., that the church in which he
was baptized is *not* in the parish of St. Remigius (see
above).   This is true, it is not so now ; but the fact is
that all the parish divisions had been changed in 1810
—hence the mistake.

It has been stated in a French biography that his
first opera was published in 1795, consequently when he
was twenty-five years old ; and hence the reader is led
to believe that Beethoven, too shy to let any one see his
work, did not appear before this time as a composer.
This notion is erroneous.   He began his musical studies
with his father at the age of four.   When, later on, he

had a music-master, who died in 1780, Beethoven, then ten years old, composed and published a funeral cantata, 'In memoriam.' The cantata, however, is not now to be found, and the fact is scarcely to be regretted ; for, however important, and even now barely comprehended, his later works may be, there is not a composer known whose first essays have not been mere childish insignificant trials, not excepting even Mozart's Babies' Sonatas, with which, quâ Sonatas, a great fuss has been made, because composed by a mere child. But then, any man who impartially reads them must admit that they discover rather the baby than the sonata. Yet, very well known is a set of variations composed, " par un amateur L. v. B., âgé de 10 ans." This is really his Opus No. 1. But he was at the age of ten already not only a proficient pianist, but an organist of such talent, that when his organ-master Neefe was appointed to another position he left Beethoven as his substitute, the deputy-organist being then ten and a half years old ; and so successful that his master said, " If the boy continues as he begins he will be a second Mozart." In fact this is what Mozart himself said when later on (1787) Beethoven was sent to Vienna and greatly desired to receive lessons from Mozart, who for one reason or another would not consent to give them, but told Beethoven to sit down to the piano and play something. Suddenly Mozart interrupted him, and asked could he improvise on a theme which he would give him. Improvisation is, in fact, the true test for an artistic nature ; there a man can show what inspiration he has got, and how he can give it effect in execution.

F

The great Masters Bach and Handel were gigantic in improvisation ; and Handel in his oratorios often wrote down conventional accompaniments, leaving the performer to do as he had done—improvise. In the first quarter of this century the real great pianists, who were musicians also—which is not the case with all the pianists of our day—Cramer, Hummel, Moscheles, even Bocklet, gave public improvisations which were greatly appreciated. In our time I know only of one great pianist— d'Albert—who has a serious talent for improvisation, which comprises instantaneous inspiration, theoretical knowledge of music and composition, as well as great execution. Mozart then, no mean connoisseur, the moment he heard Beethoven play, wanted at once to find out " de quel bois il se chauffait," and gave him a *motif* for improvisation ; and so amazed and delighted was he with what he heard, that he turned round to his friends and said, " Note this boy, he will create some noise in the world." And we know that he did. Beethoven was then seventeen years old, and Mozart, just a few years before his premature death, was thirty-two.

A recent instance of a great faculty for improvising is the little boy Hofmann, barely ten years old ; and who is guided to such an extent by the theme given him, that he exactly continues the style which the *motif* requires, be that style Wagner or Chopin. In my biography of Mozart I stated that when fourteen years old he had composed an opera, and stood with the bâton at the conductor's desk. Well, Beethoven when twelve years and a half old filled the place which is called in Italy " maestro al cembalo," because it is the maestro who

before the orchestral rehearsals begin conducts a rehearsal of the chorus and the soloists at the piano ; and
Beethoven had a clavicymbal in the orchestra, at which
he sat and conducted the band. The custom of having
a piano placed in the orchestra for the conductor, even
when he led with the bâton, was frequent until twenty
years ago, when the conductor used to strike a chord, or
even a single note sometimes, for the singer to begin, and
give him also a few chords during the recitative. What
in those times musicians did for the love of art, without
thinking of the financial advantages to be derived from
it, is evident from the example of these two most illustrious men, Beethoven and Mozart. How the latter
sacrificed every benefit his operas or his position as
Court Composer should have brought him, and died
miserably poor, is well known ; and Beethoven's first
pay when appointed real organist (at the age of thirteen)
was £13 a year, or exactly five shillings a week—little
more than a man-servant usually gets per day. And
yet it was somewhat better pay than Verdi received in
a similar position and at a similar age when he was
appointed organist, and had moreover to make the
journey to and fro on foot.

It is well known that Beethoven became deaf ; and
after having for some time used a brass ear-trumpet, he
found that it affected his brain, and he took to using a
slate, on which those who conversed with him had to write
their answers. He had the queerest ideas imaginable
about the origin of his deafness, and persistently pretended that the doctors knew nothing at all about it, and
that they had treated him all wrong, and that the real

seat of the evil was by no means in the ear, but in the
stomach ! He used to be attended to by a sort of
housekeeper, whom, however, he often sent on errands.
It therefore happened sometimes that visitors rang and
knocked without the slightest result, because he did not
hear them. Sometimes they simply opened one door
after the other until they found themselves in his presence, he being made aware of their arrival either by
seeing them, or, when his face was not turned towards
the door, by the sensation of their treading the floor.
He then instantly came forward, with his slate in hand,
to begin the conversation in the only way possible for
the poor man. One of these visitors gave me, many years
ago, a description of what the room looked like in which
Beethoven wrote his immortal scores. The ceiling was
rather low, but the room was a large one, with a big
square table in the middle, which was covered with
books of all shapes and sizes, papers, music, a large
repeater watch, his ear-trumpet, small memorandum-
books in quantities, partly written on, some yet containing rough sketches of a few bars, etc. ; an inkstand, an
innumerable quantity of pencils of different colours,
music-paper both long and wide, and any amount of
musical sketches and other things. To the left stood
his bed, covered with music printed and in manuscript ;
the window-sills seemed to be made of common wood
without any paint on. On one of them a big nail
served as a support for a fiddle and bow ; and my in-
formant observed that the wood of the window-frames
was covered with little pencil-writings, partly music, and
partly short observations. On several chairs about lay

what most likely at a recent visit a laundress had deposited there—a number of shirts, white, starched very stiff, and one or two with *jabots*, the fashion of that day.

The inhabitants of Vienna have often with pardonable pride boasted that their city was the preferred sojourn of so many great composers—Haydn, Mozart, Gluck, Beethoven, Schubert, etc. But it was not the liberality of the Viennese which rendered their city especially desirable to those geniuses. Mozart made so little money that he had to borrow in order to live, and when he was offered by the King of Prussia a very liberal annuity in Berlin, he tendered his resignation and went to take leave of the Emperor. But it was quite sufficient for the latter to say " What, Mozart, can you leave me ? " " No," said Mozart, " no, your Majesty ; I will stay." And stay he did. Yet without any help or increase of his income ; and he died deeply in debt. Beethoven, who had for pupil no less exalted a personage than the Cardinal Archduke Rudolph, told the Cardinal that he was afraid he would be obliged to leave Vienna, in order to make sufficient money honourably to live upon. Hearing this, the Archduke seemed to be quite beside himself, and proposed instantly to speak to the Princes Esterhazy, Razumovski, etc., so as to make up a subscription and keep Beethoven in Vienna. And he did speak to these personages ; but when Beethoven, having been promised an amply sufficient annuity, depended on their contributions, one after the other stopped, for one reason or another—now for sudden losses, then because it was thought that the contribution was only expected for a while ; *summa summarum*—great cry, little wool.

To what an extent the great man, usually represented as being haughty, ill-humoured, and quite a bear, could be kind and cordial and amiable, may be gathered from a letter addressed from Vienna by Louis Schloesser, the eminent Darmstadt Court Conductor, to a friend in Germany. Therein he tells that, having been introduced to Beethoven in November, 1822, after a performance of 'Fidelio,' with Mme. Schroeder in the title rôle, Beethoven asked him what he had written (Schloesser was then twenty-two years old), and told him to bring some of his manuscripts on a certain day and remain to dinner. But on the very day, while Schloesser was just looking through the MSS. which he was to take to the terrible judge, his door opened, and in walked Beethoven, saying that as it was a very fine day he came to take the young man for a constitutional before dinner, and had for the purpose come up the fourth floor in the Hotel zum Erzherzog Carl, where Schloesser * then lived, and Beethoven at that time was fifty-two years of age. Kindness is not so much shown in the cost of presents, as in the way of presenting them ; there is, as a German proverb says, much honour in a glass of wine ; which means that a gentle nature will show much more in the way ·

* Court-conductor Louis Schloesser died in November, 1886, in his eighty-seventh year. He was the father of the eminent musician, Mr. Adolphus Schloesser, to whose obliging kindness I owe a copy of Beethoven's autograph manuscript which is attached to next page. It represents part of a letter addressed to Mr. Schloesser, sen., by Beethoven himself.

to oblige, than in the magnitude of the gift, which may depend on the means of the giver and not on his heart-felt wish to oblige you. If a man be able to give a sovereign as a charity, but will throw the gold coin so as to avoid the touch of the needy person, he will by humiliating him diminish the value of the gift; but it is given only to few people—to gentlewomen, above all—to accompany the gift with a warm sympathetic look or smile, or a kind word, which will do more than the gift itself to console and comfort.

Side by side, then, the great man of the day and the young composer walked about till they came home to dinner; and the opinion which, after careful perusal, Beethoven gave of the manuscripts submitted to him for judgment, and the remarks he made concerning his own way of writing, are too interesting to be withheld from the reader. His expressions show the encouraging kindness of a great man where he sees promising and rising talent, and at the same time he shows himself honestly critical in the interest of the artist himself.

In this case the artist was deeply thankful, although for truth, however kindly intended, people are not always grateful ; and, as a rule, wounded vanity is all you meet with, instead of the respectful modesty with which Mr. Schloesser accepted the good advice tendered him.

"I have been pleased," said Beethoven, "with your work, and am happy to say this is no pupil's effort. The score shows that you assume a position in the centre of your band, that you know the effect of each instrument and its practical use. I like the structure and the form, of which you show yourself fully master. Light and shade are well distributed between voices and instruments, and you know how to lend to the whole picture a warm and attractive colour. This is the praiseworthy part which I fully acknowledge ; but there are other points with which I agree less, and which I am going to tell you. There is much that appears fidgety, too stormy, not steady enough. Your imagination runs away with you. I miss the careful concentration of your ideas, which follow each other without being properly linked together. You should not lavish your thoughts to right and left, but contrive to lead them up to a climax or anti-climax. Instead of giving so much, you should have given less, and you would have produced more symmetry and a more homogeneous style. But that is the fault of heaven-storming youth, that has head and heart at boiling heat, and always thinks there is never enough done. Time will cure this exuberance, and I prefer, at any rate, to see too much creative power, than to find mere empty conventionality."

The young man stood trembling and thankful for the care with which that mighty genius had evidently read and judged his efforts, and he naturally ventured to ask what he had best do, and in what way Beethoven's genius had led him from the first to such high flight. " Oh, I bear my ideas," said Beethoven, " very long with me in my brain ere I attempt to write them down, and I can depend upon my memory that I never forget a phrase which has taken hold of my mind. Sometimes I change some parts, I entirely condemn others, and then I try again until I think I have found the right way, with which at last I am satisfied myself. But then begins in my head the working out in width, in breadth, and height, without ever losing my hold on the funda- mental idea, which grows and grows and increases until the whole picture stands complete before my mind's eye —then I need only sit down and write it out, which, once begun, I do quickly and steadily, as I may find time to do it ; because I usually work at different things at the same time, but, as I told you, without ever confusing one with the other. Perhaps you may ask, where do I take my ideas from ? That is more than I can say. The ideas come, and there they are ; sometimes so palpable that I fancy I can put my hands upon them while I am out in the meadows or in the forest, at sunrise, or while I lie sleepless in bed, as the mood may seize me. The inspiration with a poet would come in words, whereas to me it comes in tones that sing, shout, storm, or sigh sweetly, until at last they take quiet form in notes ; then when I have written them down I become calm again, and look at my work, and turn it and mend it until I am satisfied."

This description of the way in which the greatest genius of this century produced his work—a description given by himself, simply and naturally—proves that, although the real reason of the powerful effect which his grand ideas produce upon us lies in the inspiration of genius, which, like the course of the stars in the spheres, we can see and calculate and yet not conceive, it is never-theless the severe self-criticism which great men exert upon their own work, never satisfied until they reach the highest point which it is possible to attain, that renders their work so far superior to that of mediocrity, for mediocrity is not only quite pleased and contented with any common idea, but even disdains taking the trouble of refining and polishing ; a trouble which the great masters in poetry, in painting, in music, have always most industriously taken. The astonishing fact has often been told how Mozart had written no overture to his opera 'Don Giovanni' till the last day, when he sat down to a glass of punch, and, talking to his wife, wrote it all in a few hours. Yet that is just what he did. But he did not then compose it; he only wrote down what he had weeks before composed, turned over in his mind, scratched out, replaced and refitted, until the whole formed in his mind the picture he wanted. When that was done, he took the pen and devoted a few hours to the mere mechanical work of writing it out, just as a stenographer would do with his shorthand MS. when he has to transcribe it for the reader. The work is before his mind's eye, he only expresses it in legible signs. This is the way great composers have often kept the work in their brain, and, only when the right moment came, copied it out on paper. Italian composers have rarely taken that trouble. Trusting more to the spontaneous flow of melody than to elaborate figures of counter-point, etc., many of them sat down, allowed the ideas to flow into their pens, and quickly wrote down their singing thoughts ; so quickly, indeed, that sometimes in a few weeks a whole operatic score was improvised.

Beethoven was nineteen years old when the first great French Revolution convulsed all Europe. The past tumbled to pieces, and the present was a surging mass—a chaos, in which the germ of a great future, the liberty of thought and freedom for all, was barely recognisable. The storm which passed over traditions and time-honoured rights and titles passed not only over France, but it was on the point of upsetting and devastating the whole continent of Europe. And not in politics alone, but in art also, the latter years of the last century had become of unusual importance. Gluck and Mozart, the giants of music, died between 1785 and 1795 ; Haydn created and firmly established the symphony and the quartet. Important creations of every kind were in the air. The greatest hero of modern times conquered for himself the Marshal's bâton, and, leaning on this short but mighty support, seated himself on the throne of France, and at the head of his cohorts dictated the law to the Universe. These events made a deep impression on Beethoven's fiery nature, on his refined but passionate republican organization ; and it is well known that he composed a Symphony which he called 'Bonaparte.' This work he had been requested to write by Marshal Bernadotte, who in 1798 was French Ambassador at the Court of Vienna. He agreed to do so with all the more eagerness that he felt an unbounded admiration for the First Consul of the French Republic.

The Symphony was simply superscribed " 'Bonaparte' —Luigi van Beethoven " ; but when Bonaparte added the crown of Cæsar to the laurels of the imperator, Beethoven, whose ideal had been republican freedom, scratched out the name and called it ' Sinfonia Eroica.'

Beethoven remembered the Marshal very well twenty-five years later, when (March 1, 1823) he had finished his great 'Missa Solemnis,' and wrote to Bernadotte, then King of Sweden, to thank him for a nomination to the Swedish Academy, and asked him to subscribe fifty ducats for a copy of the Mass.

From what has been stated in the foregoing pages it is clear that Beethoven's character was a mixture of passionate temper and kindheartedness, even to tenderness. The following story of the spider proves both sides. When a child a violin was given to Beethoven, on which he practised and learned the elements of execution. Yet even in those days he was quite capable of giving himself up to an idea, and a long-drawn Andante cantabile fascinated his mother, who listened to his studies with a friend of hers—an old lady of the neighbourhood. But not only these two kindly-disposed souls, but, Orpheus-like, another inferior soul was attracted by his bow. A spider weaving its skilful though delicate trap for its daily dinner worked industriously in the corner of the ceiling until Beethoven began to play. Then it stopped work, swung itself down from the ceiling, often on the very neck of the violin, and listened. Beethoven, who at that time had not thousands of eyes hanging on his bâton, was rather pleased at and attached to this listener, who most practically proved the value it attached to the performance by risking his life in coming so near the enchanted instrument. And ill was it rewarded. The mother one day perceiving the ugly animal seized and killed it. But the boy Beethoven was so put out and so miserable at losing his strange auditor that he burst into tears, and seizing his violin smashed it against the floor, shivering it into a thousand pieces.

When Beethoven was first sent to Vienna he was only fifteen years old, but there his talent of organist and improvisator found speedy acknowledgment. He made the acquaintance of those magnates whose names he immortalized by dedicating his works to them—such as Prince Lichnowsky, Count Waldstein, Prince Razumofsky, and his famous pupil the brother of the Emperor Francis, Archduke Rudolph, a Cardinal, and a distinguished amateur himself.

He gratefully accepted from Prince Lichnowsky a pension of six hundred gulden, amounting to about £60 of our money; but it must be remembered that a hundred years ago one could live liberally in Vienna on five pounds a month, whereas now that would barely suffice for a week. It will readily be observed that republicans like Beethoven and Wagner, who in early youth were banished from their country for revolutionary ideas and for fighting against the powers that be, yet kindly allowed aristocratic patrons to pay their debts and support them in adversity. Beethoven even lived very much in aristocratic society in Vienna, where he was well paid for his lessons, and where he acquired the sinews of war so necessary for a man, whatever his political principles may be. I am convinced, however, that, just as he did not disdain the money of aristocrats, and as Richard Wagner allowed the King of Bavaria freely to open his purse for the quondam Barricadist, neither *because* it came, nor *although* it came, from a Prince, just so did Beethoven fall in love with several Countesses, not because nor although they were Countesses, but simply because they were ladies ; and he was so impressionable on that count, that it may well be said of him, that he remained faithful only to one lady, his Muse. The story of his falling in love with his pupil, the Countess Giulietta Guicciardi, and his pretended jealous rage at her marrying the well-known Count Gallenberg, is, to the best of my belief, idle, though universally circulated talk, based upon his having dedicated to her one of his most popular sonatas, that in C minor, known by the sobriquet ' The Moonlight,' nobody knows why. I knew her when she was an old lady and had a son, Hector, a little older than I. She spoke with no great admiration of Beethoven as a master. She said that he was frightfully *emporté,* and did not mind hitting her on the shoulder, and on one particular occasion so violently that she could not wear a low dress in the evening. So far as I was able to judge at that distance of time, it seemed to me that she, having been a tall, proud, beautiful girl (clear traces of which could still be detected when Beethoven had been more than twenty-five years dead), he fell in love with her, as he fell in love with nearly every handsome girl he met. But I do not think that there was on her part the remotest idea of a passion, or even a tender attachment for him, and therefore there is not the slightest cause for accusation of jealousy on his part when she married. She was a poor Italian girl, and the Count Gallenberg, who was a composer of ballet music, and came much in contact in the Imperial Opera House with Italian ladies, was rather struck by her majestic appearance, and though he was far from rich himself, he made himself agreeable, and she took him, as most pretty but poor and respectable girls would take what is called *un mari sortable.*

It may seem curious that I should appear to take so much trouble to prove that the generally, I may say universally accredited reason for his dedicating the C minor Sonata to Giulietta Guicciardi has no romance to rest upon, and was by no means a love affair. But the basis of the whole supposition is a letter which his friend Holz discovered in a secret drawer—a letter written by Beethoven himself without date, without the name of the place whence written, nor an indication to whom it was addressed ; but *supposed* to be addressed to the Countess Gallenberg *née* Guicciardi. It is not quite clear why a letter written to her had not been sent off, and if it was one of his numerous love vagaries, what does such an epistle prove ? Schindler says that Beethoven confessed to him that he loved her for seven months, the longest duration of any passion he ever felt. Moreover was that letter said to be a reply to one of hers dated 1806, whereas the Countess was married on October 3rd, 1803. The few lessons she took were given to her when single in 1801, and it was then he dedicated to her the so-called Moonlight Sonata. (Beethoven's own words as written on this Op. 27 are: "Sonata quasi fantasia dedicata alla Madamigella Contessa Giulietta di Guicciardi.") If his confession goes for anything, his love lasted only a few months; but how can this be reconciled with the letter written three years after her wedding, and therefore some four or five years after his teaching the young lady? I think it is a pity to drag everything that a great man did into the light of public discussion. A man may be a very great composer and yet a flirt. Examples are not wanting even in our own days.

Rossini, who had always *le mot pour rire*, used to say: "In our time, we endeavoured to make music for the brain and for the ears; but it seems to me that, nowadays, people are quite content when the thing looks well." This, I feel confident, was often his guiding opinion. For instance, when Meyerbeer prepared 'The Huguenots,' his lawyer and *coréligionnaire* Crémieux gave a luncheon, where he invited some influential friends to meet Meyerbeer. Rossini, one of the guests, never ate a bit. Madame Crémieux, with the lynx eyes of a hostess who has round her table people invited for a meal, suddenly pounced upon her abstemious friend with that question which every lady imagines must go straight to the heart of her guests: "I am sure, Monsieur Rossini, you don't like that dish; one cannot easily please such a fine connoisseur as you are." "Pardon, madame, that

is not at all the reason, but I never eat between my
breakfast and my dinner. Of course, you will ask me
why, then, did I come to a luncheon party? I will tell
you. The other day I was invited to hear a performance
of my 'William Tell' overture. At the moment where
the allegro begins, I saw two men in the band putting
their trumpets up, but I could not, for the life of me,
hear one note ; so I asked the manager why they did
not play. 'Oh, that is very simple,' he said ; 'I could
not get two trumpeters, but I thought I'd get some men
to hold up the trumpet. It always looks well to see
trumpets in an orchestra ; but, of course, as they can't
play, you can't hear them.' Now, I can't eat any more
than they could play ; but, as Meyerbeer, who is so
superstitious, would have taken it for a bad omen if I
had sent an excuse, I thought I would just sit behind
my plate, because it looks well to have old friends sit
down round one's table."

Rossini, you see, did not seem to be a vain man, although I will not say whether he was or was not. Beethoven, who certainly had every right to be so, never took
the trouble to hide his feelings on that sore point, and
when his ire was aroused—and that was more easily done
than to keep it down—he expressed himself unhesitat-
ingly, and very clearly indeed. So you can see at Heili-
genstadt, near Vienna, where they are now forming a sort
of Beethoven Museum, like the Mozarteum at Salzburg, a
sketch of a *château* in Nether Austria, where a few years
before his death Beethoven used to compose, notably one
of his so-called posthumous quartets. The ground where
that castle was built belonged to Beethoven's brother, a

G

chemist, who had made some money, and was rather fond of displaying his wealth. He called upon his illustrious brother, and left a card, upon which he had engraved his name: "Jean von Beethoven, landed proprietor." This assumed title so enraged Beethoven that he deliberately went to call upon his brother when he knew he would not be at home, and left his card: "Louis von Beethoven, brain proprietor."

A great man like Beethoven, not only great in the same way as others, who simply distinguish themselves in their art or their profession—hundreds of whom are always to be found in any great city—but a genius who broke the traditions of the past, and all its established rules, to become, as it were, a legislator in art and create new laws and say, "Thus it shall be, because I say so;" such a great man can, with regard to his character, be best understood by what directly emanates from himself, his words spoken or written.

Buffon's saying, "Le style c'est l'homme," is well known; but to study Beethoven in his letters is to know him in the different and varying qualities which, like the facets of a diamond, his character showed. Rough in appearance, but with an excellent heart, kind and generous to his friends, yet careful to earn money by his works, such he proves himself in the following letters, which speak for themselves. The first is addressed to his friend Ries, the second to his publisher, Hofmeister, at Leipzig.

"Enclosed I send you a letter addressed to Count Browne. I ask him to let you have my 59 ducats (£23 10s.). I must reproach you for not having told

me long ago. Am I not your true friend? Why hide
your wants from me? None of my friends must want
so long as I have anything."

No. 2: "Are you all together ridden by the devil?
(Reitet Euch alle der Teufel?) How can you propose
to me to write such a Sonata? Here is my reply *pres-
tissimo.* The lady may have the piece written entirely
according to her own æsthetic plan by paying 5 ducats
(£2) for the sole right of performance and her exclusive
property for one year, but she must not allow any one
to copy or publish it, nor shall I touch it for that lapse
of time. After that year it is mine, and I shall publish
it. If she thinks it an honour, she may have it dedicated to her. The Lord bless you. In my quartets are
published so many mistakes that they swim about like
fish in a pond. Questo è un piacere per un autore,[1] that
is what they call engraving. Really I feel as if the
graver was passing over my very skin. Think of me
as I think of you. L. v. B."

It has been often observed that Beethoven, when
asked why he denied being a pupil of Haydn, replied:
"I deny it not, but I have never learned anything from
him. He never would correct my mistakes." Yet
when, the day after the production of his ballet music
to Prometheus, he met Haydn in the street, the old man
said to him: "I heard your music last night. I liked it
very well." To which Beethoven, alluding to Haydn's
Oratorio, replied, "Oh, dear master (lieber Meister), it
is far from being a *creation*" (Es ist noch lange keine

---

[1] That is a real pleasure for the composer.

Schöpfung).   " And never will be," said Haydn, without
any mock modesty.   Altogether the relations were not
pleasant between these great musicians, the older one
resenting, and perhaps not unnaturally so, an allusion
uncalled for to his immensely successful Oratorio in
comparison with a work which not only had far more
modest pretensions, but was the work of a young man
who had not yet been recognised to be the Hercules he
proved to be in later years.

The kind judgment of contemporaries on great
musicians has never been more fully illustrated than in
Beethoven's case.   A Leipzig paper said of his first
symphonies :   " There is a certain Beethoven who has
written some sonatas for the piano which, though not
great works, are neither incorrect nor bad music.   Why
cannot he be contented with what he understands, and
why must he go and write for the orchestra, which he
understands not ? "

From a much more authorized source comes this
amusingly incorrect judgment :   " He (Beethoven) never
would (?) dive into the mysteries of counterpoint.   Had
he done so, his imaginative vein as well as his creative
genius might have been checked."   And that was said
of the composer of the Missa in D.   And pray how can
we explain Sebastian Bach's immense creation, who did
nothing but " dive into the mysteries of counterpoint " ?
And this was written, as I said, by a competent man.
Much easier to understand is Moscheles' letter, written
at a time when Beethoven's glory had not even begun
to dawn outside his own country, and which runs thus :
" I learned from my schoolfellows that a young com-

poser had appeared at Vienna, who wrote the oddest
stuff possible, such as no one could either play or understand—crazy music in opposition to all rule, and that
this composer's name was Beethoven." This was in
1804. Yet Beethoven had already been appointed
organist twenty years before, with a salary of £1 1s. 8d.
a month (that was not a time of telegraphs and railways
and rapid communication); and one can well understand that at first his music appeared "crazy," because
it broke with all tradition and struck out a new path for
itself. As to his right to soar high over the *commun des
martyrs*, nobody now disputes it; but so long as small
talent could, it strove to detract from the value of this
great man by inventing small scandals about him, going
so far as to state in a German dictionary that he was
the illegitimate son of Frederic II. At the commencement of this paper I have already given in detail his
baptismal registry, so as to leave no doubt on that
score.

He was as obstinate as his father, and had to be
driven by force to his piano, and when there would not
sit still. So much for "predestined children." I have
alluded to his pupil, Mdlle. Guicciardi; and to his other
pupil, the Cardinal Archduke Rudolph, who held him
in very high esteem. Beethoven declared that when he
had given the Archduke lessons of not less than two
and a half hours, he could do no more work for that
day. Generally speaking, teaching bored him dreadfully; and it would have been much more appropriate
to say that his imaginative or even creative power would
have suffered from *that* dry work, than from that of

counterpoint, which is not dry at all ; whereas teaching is
not only dry, but drying work in its effect on one's brain.

It is for the creator of so many standard works of
course very important to fix the movement he wished
for his works, when the designations used are not always
a sure guide. Thus, for instance, did he write on the
Allegretto of his Seventh Symphony, when a conductor,
through taking it too fast, enraged him, " Andante quasi
allegretto." As a rule, however, although the designation must give some idea, and the metronome still more
precisely the wish of the composer, I imagine that the
best plan would be to leave to an able conductor the
judgment of the *tempo* which should be chosen for such
a work of art. He may arrive at a decision not entirely
in compliance with what the composer had imagined ;
but I am not quite sure, extraordinary as the opinion
may seem, that the composer is *always* right in the
movement he assigns to his work. It may—I am far
from saying that it will often happen—but it may
happen that, coolly judging a work laid before him, a
great musician may be better able to judge what would
suit the work best. On the other hand, it is clear that
as a matter of course the composer's indication is entitled
to the greatest respect. It happened that Mozart, present
at the performance of one of his symphonies, remarked
that the conductor hurried the orchestra beyond what
had evidently been their ordinary movement. Probably,
as Mozart thought, that was done in his honour. " They
imagine," he said, " that by so doing they impart fire to
their performance ; but if there is no fire in them, they
cannot be galloped into it."

The movements and the refinement of performance require study and rehearsals : and Beethoven, when he had composed that tower of orchestral works, the Ninth Symphony, complained that he could not get sufficient rehearsals. He wanted at least three. But the Imperial Intendant, having a big ballet to put on the stage, and wanting the band for what he considered much more important, wrote on the margin of the petition, "Two rehearsals are ample." When Habeneck, after Beethoven's death, brought out his symphonies with that famous Conservatoire orchestra, composed entirely of the professors of the Institution, he rehearsed not the Ninth, which is so much longer and much more difficult, but the Fifth Symphony in C Minor for *two years*, and not one of the nine symphonies for not less than fifteen months! until he obtained a refinement of crescendos and decrescendos and a multiplicity of remarkable *nuances* that no orchestra in the world could surpass. Beethoven was very particular, clearly and circumstantially to mark all his passages exactly as he wanted them rendered ; but the performers did not always take sufficient notice of the master's lessons, and he one day got into such a fury on account of the neglect of his signs, that he said : "But the *p* and the *f* and the increasing and decreasing signs stand there for some reason ? As you play it I might as well scratch out all the indications I have given, and it would not be more feelingless, unimpressive, and monotonous!"

Beethoven got up to work sometimes at daybreak at 2 or 3 A.M. ; and being nearly always short of money, he wrote "Noten in Nöthen," which means that he

wrote musical notes in need. It is not exactly con-
ceivable, considering the very unpretending way he lived,
the quantity of music he produced, and the fair though
not brilliant prices he realized, that he had not more
money at his disposal, for the depredations of his spoilt
nephew did not amount to very big sums. He had
made a certain scale of prices, as follows:

Symphony for Orchestra	£20–25*
Overtures	guineas 8–12
A Quartet	£16
A Quintet	20
A Septet	24
A Violin Concerto with Orchestra. . .	20
A Pianoforte ditto	24
A Sonata	12
A Grand Sonata	16
An Opera Seria or an Oratorio . . .	120
A Requiem	48
Six Songs with Pianoforte Accompaniment .	8
Six short Songs	5†

Under all these manuscripts Beethoven wrote: "Copy-
right for France and England reserved, and prices
occasionally to be altered."

Although Beethoven had, so to say, created the
orchestral resources, powerfully using and enlarging the
sonority, and inventing through his profound knowledge
and the intuition of his genius a whole tone-palette new
to the century, he always advocated and foresaw further

* Wagner received from the American ladies who wished for
their Centenary celebration an orchestral march, 5,000 dollars, a
little over £1,000.
† Sullivan received for one song, £700 down.

improvement, saying, "As yet the limit has not been reached where man can say, *Non plus ultra !* Truth is the veiled statue: no mortal man hath uplifted that veil." Perhaps he alluded to Schiller's veiled image at Sais which everybody wanted to see, yet were not allowed to touch the veil of. One young man, more reckless and more daring, entered the temple and proceeded to the statue, bent on the outrage, when the priest warned him away. "Why," said the young man, "should I not satisfy my desire for knowledge when nothing separates me from that satisfaction but a veil so light for my fingers——" "And a law," interrupted the priest, "that weighs tons for your conscience." "Never mind the law," said the young man, and he lifted up the veil, and, so goes the legend, he fell down unconscious, and long remained so ; and when at last he was brought to he exclaimed plaintively, "Let no one dare and discover truth through guilty means ; it will bring him no luck," and he suffered agony, and died at last in deep misery. If Beethoven meant the great secret of creation and life, the great answer to the eternal why ?—the inexplicable secret how a grain of seed scarcely perceivable to the naked eye holds in itself the germ of the rose, and another one that of the tulip, and invariably develops into that which it had been—if, in two words, he meant the veil which the created never can lift from the Creative power, he may well say no mortal man can unveil it, and mad he who tries to attain the unattainable.

Beethoven had a great admiration for Schubert, and I know that he said it was a thousand pities that Rossini did not learn more, as he would have done great things ; but whether it is true that Rossini called four times on Beethoven and he would never receive him, I cannot say. I never heard Rossini speak of him except with the greatest veneration ; and it must be remembered that Rossini's latest and greatest work, 'William Tell,' was brought out after Beethoven's death. Beethoven wrote loads of letters, very carelessly some of them ; and he had an unfortunate mania of writing in languages with which he was but very imperfectly acquainted. Seyfried said Beethoven knew Latin, French, and Italian. Perhaps so. But how he wrote it you must not ask. There is a certain letter of his held by the firm of Broadwood, written in French, it is difficult to understand why, seeing that Mr. Broadwood would have much better understood his German. But there is also another letter known, in French, the beginning of which I will here copy ; and the reader will agree with me, that the most astonishing part of the affair is, that, knowing how superficial was his knowledge, he should not have asked a friend to write it for him. " L'amitié de vous envers moi me pardonnerà touts le fault contrè la langue Francaises, etc." For the English people he had a great admiration, for his two great wants, love and money, were more likely to be satisfied here. So he wrote to Ries : " I commend my-self to your wife and to all the fair Englishwomen who consent to receive my greetings." But although he had a very inflammable heart indeed, he did not encourage love made to him where he was not the originator of the romance. A Mrs. Halm wrote to him when he had already lived half a century, and most sentimentally

asked him for a souvenir—if possible, a lock of his hair
—and he was cruel enough to cut some grey hair from
a goat and to send it to her in a locket which she had
transmitted to him for the purpose. There would not
have been much harm in it, because Mrs. Halm in perfect good faith wore the locket ; and since it is faith
only that renders you happy, she, thinking that she wore
the cherished hair on her heart, was happy. But after
her delusion had lasted for years, a friend of Beethoven
to whom he had laughingly confided the whole story,
cruelly revealed the secret to the very lady who was
the victim of the hoax, and she with bitter tears wrote
to Beethoven, telling him how cruel it was to take such
unfair advantage of her admiration for, and her unbounded good faith in him, and to render a friend, a
sincere adorer, if she might say so, ridiculous before all
her friends, to whom she had often shown the relic with
all veneration possible, and now it came out that it was
all a goat's hair. She pleaded her case so well, that
Beethoven, touched by her resignation—she did not
cry for vengeance, but submitted meekly—repented of
his joke, and sent her some of his real venerable grey
hair, which made her happy. *Ce que femme veut Dieu le
veut.* Have you ever known an exception to the rule ?
It is just because they always pose as victims that they
excite our pity and adroitly make us the weaker sex,
and we have always to do their will.

Beethoven was not in the beginning of his career, nor
even in the middle of it, recognised as the immense
genius he was, because people could not understand him.
He spread his wings, and they could not follow ; yet

when he died they knew they had lost one of the greatest men of their time. The eagle that flies near the sun must be contented not to be followed by the birds *minorum gentium*; and it is the invariable misfortune of genius to fly too high, too fast, with too powerful wings to be followed, still less reached and understood, by weaker conceptions, who want time, leisure, and patient study to conceive, understand, and appreciate the mind whose force has risen above the level of all contemporaries.

Beethoven died on March 26 in the year 1827. His agony was long, and he died after a fearful struggle. A tremendous storm broke over the town, as if the elements wished to bear witness, by an extraordinary cataclysm, to the great loss humanity was on the point of sustaining. His funeral took place on the 29th of the same month amid general mourning ; the (then) greatest living poet of Austria, Grillparzer, had written a funeral oration, and Anschütz, the greatest tragedian of the Court Theatre, delivered it in eloquent and deeply moving language ; and yet when it came to the point of writing him an epitaph on his marble stone, nobody found anything grander, more eloquent in its conciseness than that only word :

" BEETHOVEN " !

Hard and struggling as his death was his life, and so was the process of creating the immortal works, which only after sixty years we are able fully to appreciate. His sketch-books show the labour of the simplest idea. Thrown down on paper, changed, re-written, again changed, never satisfying the genius who exercised so severely what is most necessary for the production of great works, namely, self-criticism ; until the composition was above the smallest fault-finding, content only when the master-work stood there complete, and not a spot could be discovered, even through the sharp glasses of his own criticism.

Beethoven has written for many solo instruments, for small *ensembles*, and for whole orchestras. His sonatas and concertos are a permanent model and school from which to learn. He has written too for the voice, but he treated it very often like instruments. There are none of his songs nor his operas so popular as his orchestral works ; but his symphonies—those nine colossal statues that have been compared to the Nine Muses —will for ever bear the dome of immortality, in which those who wish to do honour to art and its great priest will with deep veneration pronounce the name of " Ludwig van Beethoven."

Arthur Sullivan.

Sir Arthur Sullivan.

SUPERSTITION may be wrong. The devoutly believing ones call it sinful to believe in anything but the decision of Providence. The unbelieving ones, on the contrary, tax the superstitious with believing too much. But when one comes to think of what is possible and what may be called impossible, where is the mind bold enough who would dare to give a decision one way or another? What the Greeks called fate, what the Middle Ages called the Lord's judgment, what we may call accident, they all tend to the one terrible power, unknown and inscrutable, that decides and conceals from us the future even of the very nearest hour—a power we have to bow to whether we understand it or not, just as we calculate with the utmost precision the rotation and appearance or disappearance of all the worlds in the spheres, without even being able to conceive the distances which we so accurately calculate.

Among the superstitions noted generally are certain years when the most excellent wine grows, when the most famous men are born, and other devices more or less reliable. In 1842, two of the greatest stars on the musical horizon were created: Arthur Sullivan and Adelina Patti. Unprecedented is the success of both; unprecedented is their glory; unprecedented is the golden reward which rains upon Danaë from Jupiter-public. Luck—that is the word, so often used as an explanation of the unusual success of any man, because it is so consoling for jealous, envious, would-be rivals, not to admit the superior genius, or the greater knowledge, or the more amiable qualities of character, while just the very combination of all these qualities is required to lift on the high pedestal of contemporaneous recognition the performer, the composer, the poet, or the statesman.

Arthur Sullivan, born on May 13th, 1842 (see again the superstition that the 13th brings ill-luck), consequently now about 48 years of age, was predestined, if embracing the musical career, to excel in it, for his blood from the father's (an excellent bandmaster) side is Irish, whereas from the mother's side it is Italian. He was a wonderful child, although not a wonder-child, and he owes to serious prolonged study under the best masters as much advancement towards his high position as to the natural gifts, without which all learning can lead to nothing; for this must be well borne in mind, that it it wants a great sculptor to make an immortal bust of a block of Carrara marble, yet it wants the pure, spotless marble from which to make a masterpiece of sculpture. The effect which an eminent pianist will produce on a Steinway grand will certainly beat that which a little schoolgirl will make on the same piano, but it equally wants the instrument which responds to all the intentions of the performer, who could, for instance, not play a sonata on a dining-room table, however great his skill. It ought, therefore, to be well borne in mind that both natural gift and solid study are necessary to reach a great result, and that a man gifted with a very musical organization without knowledge of composition, orchestration, etc., will never do anything grand in music; but equally must it be understood that music cannot be learned, and that whoever has no ideas, no inspiration, no melody, can learn the rules, the laws according to which his ideas are to be treated, but if he have no ideas, he has the dress without the body to it, the piano without the inspired performer, and paper and ink and grammar without the brain to put ideas down. That is why you so often hear in England of an excellent musician who has learned the orthography, the syntaxis, the style, and who, on the strength of what he has learned, became a Doctor of Music, but his compositions, operas, or oratorios fail to please or to attract the public, because study can only develop the faculty of expressing ideas with effect, but the ideas must be there, just as the most elaborate mining apparatus will bring no gold to light where there is no ore.

Sullivan—born with that rich mine of ideas, both deep and light, grave and melodious, having begun his musical productions with one of the severest forms of composition, a quartet, having composed glees and hymns, oratorios and opéras-comiques, songs and overtures, and, save the mark! successful in all—is one of those rare born geniuses who, from the first, have given the measure of their power, and have, through a long series of works, maintained and fortified their glory. His father, as I said, was bandmaster, and quite a little fellow Arthur was when he appealed to the different members of that band to teach him each his instrument;

and at eight years, not much higher than the clarionet, he performed his part with the band. He entered the choir of the Chapel Royal, and was taught by Mr. Helmore, Chaplain-in-Ordinary to the Queen. After eighteen months' study he was able to write an anthem, submitted to Sir George Smart, who was so pleased with it that he directed it to be sung in the Chapel Royal, where Dr. Blomfield, the Bishop of London, heard it, and, inquiring the name of the composer, presented him with the first half-sovereign, the predecessor of the long row of sovereigns to follow. At the age of fourteen, whilst still at the Chapel Royal, he gained the Mendelssohn Scholarship, and was placed by the Committee in the Royal Academy of Music, where he had for teachers Sterndale Bennett and John Goss. His voice broke at sixteen, and he was sent as Mendelssohn's Scholar for three years to Leipsic, there to study composition under Rietz, counterpoint under Hauptmann, piano under Moscheles and Plaidy.

This, as you see, meant business, and he began composing in good earnest by writing for the "Öffentliche Prüfung" (public examination) an overture, 'The Light of the Harem,' and a String Quartet of such merit that it was shown to Spohr, who looked with amazement at the young fellow, and asked him, "So jung und schön, so weit in der Kunst?" (Such a mere lad, and already so advanced in art?). Then he wrote, in rapid succession, success after success; and this is the list of his works as they followed each other: 1862, 'Tempest' (performed at the Crystal Palace) and 'The Sapphire Necklace'; 1863, 'The Enchanted Isle' (ballet performed at Covent Garden) and his only Symphony in E (performed at the Crystal Palace); 1864, a Cantata, 'Kenilworth' (produced at the Birmingham Musical Festival); 1866, Overture, 'In Memoriam,' for the Norwich Festival, and 'Cox and Box.' On these two, one of the saddest and one of the merriest of his compositions, I shall have something to say presently. In the same year he wrote a Concerto for the violoncello (performed by Piatti) and 'The Contrabandista'; 1867, an Overture, 'Marmion,' for the Philharmonic Society; 1868, 'The Prodigal Son,' for Worcester; 1869, an Overture di Ballo, for Birmingham; 1871, 'On Shore and Sea,' for the opening of the Kensington Exhibition; 1872, Te Deum for the recovery of the Prince of Wales; in 1872, too, he wrote 'Thespis' for Toole, which ran a hundred nights; 1873, an Oratorio 'The Light of the World,' for Birmingham; in 1875 came the 'Trial by Jury' and 'The Zoo'; 1877, 'The Sorcerer'; 1878, 'H.M.S. Pinafore'; 1880, 'The Pirates of Penzance,' and, for the Leeds Festival, the Sacred Drama, 'The Martyr of Antioch'; 1881, 'Patience'; 1882, 'Iolanthe'; 1884, 'Princess Ida'; 1885, 'The Mikado,' which not only made the tour of the world, but is even now given in several continental towns three or four times a week; 1886, his great masterpiece, the Oratorio 'The Golden Legend,' which was put to the severest test this autumn at a festival where the town was split into two distinct camps, one who favoured the Conductor engaged, and one who stuck to the Organist of the town, who was not engaged, as he had expected; so that the whole of the followers of the Organist severally stayed away from the Festival altogether, and the performances made very poor receipts indeed, except one day, when 'The Golden Legend' was given; then Montagues and Capulets flocked to the hall, which was filled to overflowing, and the receipts reached the highest possible sum. In 1887, 'Ruddigore,' and 1888, 'The Yeoman of the Guard,' close for the moment this brilliant array of successes, in which I have not included his numerous popular songs, at the head of which stands 'The Lost Chord,' a truly magnificent song, of which over 180,000 copies have been sold; and 'Let me dream again,' dedicated to Madame Nilsson, and which, with many others, yields a magnificent income of royalty.

I mentioned two works with merry and sad incidents above, both belonging to the same year. When in 1866, that is when he was twenty-four years old, and had a commission to write for the Norwich Festival, he could not find an appropriate subject, and said to his father, to whom he was devotedly attached: "I have a mind to give up this whole affair, I don't know what to choose for a subject." Don't do that, my boy," said the father; "don't give it up, something will happen that may furnish you with an opportunity." And three days afterwards something did happen—his father suddenly died. Remember what I said in the beginning of this notice anent superstition. Half mad with grief, his son followed the coffin to the grave, and when he came home and sat with his mother, brooding over his loss, he suddenly jumped up and said: "Mother, I can't bear it. I must cry out my grief in music." And there and then he sat down and wrote. And thus was the overture 'In Memoriam' created. Another and much more cheerful

opportunity, and one of historical interest, was the evening when he saw Du Maurier and Harold Power perform
Offenbach's farce 'Les deux Aveugles.' It instantly
stimulated him to try his hand on a similar exhilarating
work, and leaving the party with Burnand, the genial
editor of *Punch*, he asked him for a libretto for a similar
production. Burnand proposed 'Cox and Box.' Sullivan
instantly accepted, but, like other great composers, he
deferred writing the score from week to week until, the
work being announced, the last week arrived, when he
had promised to conduct the performance on Saturday.
He diligently wrote and got copied the score, but when
Friday came the last half was not written. So on Friday
night at eight o'clock he got two copyists to sit up with
him, and while he scored they copied until seven in the
morning; then they broke down, and there were yet
three numbers to be written and copied. In despair
Sullivan wrote these last numbers in the orchestral parts
only, not having time to write the score, finished at
eleven, took a bath, at twelve he rehearsed at the theatre,
and at two the performance began—everybody knows
with what success. His social position is such as not
only to be received by, but himself to receive royalty at
his house, which is furnished and provided with every
comfort that elegance, wealth, and taste can accumulate
in any set of rooms.

This is a rapid sketch of one of the most brilliant
careers known. Sir Arthur Sullivan, a composer of
immense resource, tried in all possible *genres* of musical
work—song, madrigal, opera, oratorio, symphony—has
great originality, infinite (not endless) melody, deep

knowledge of orchestration, he is a master of the form and rhythm, has musical wit, which exists just as literary wit, and a facility of writing simple, easy, and enchanting phrases. Not always serious enough for grand oratorio, now and then phrases escape him which are not by any means of a sufficiently solid style (as in 'The Martyr of Antioch'). So, too, in his operas and operettas, here and there repetitions of previous ideas, and perhaps this or that phrase of not very distinguished style, form the black point on the brilliant wing of the butterfly, which, though a small spot, brings out the other colours in still greater relief; but these are the spots in the sun, and when I have said that, in his private life he is a man of the most spotless honour, and has for many years been the sole support of his deceased brother's numerous family, whom he has most generously and liberally educated and brought up, I have said enough to explain why I hold Sir Arthur Sullivan to be one of the most celebrated and most justly admired men of this century.

For completeness sake I might as well add that 'The Gondoliers,' Sullivan's last opera, is by many considered his most successful work (perhaps because it is the last). It reminds one vividly of a young man who could not make up his mind which of two sisters he should marry, because the one he saw last appeared to him always the most attractive. One reason for this especially favourable opinion may be that in 'The Gondoliers,' Sullivan relied by no means, as he has done in some of his operas, on his great skill as a musician, but he has written an unusually great number of single pieces, duos, quartets,

and two admirable quintets. Having by the side of
a rich mine of ideas that truly English talent for
writing madrigals, he has written all told some thirty
numbers for this opera, while I very well remember
that Donizetti once told me that he never contemplated
writing more than thirteen pieces for any of his grand
operas. But then he lived in less exacting times, when
the public was not *blasé*, as they are to-day, and they
were satisfied with finding two or three melodies easily
sticking to their memory. It will always remain a
remarkable phenomenon, that a writer so successful in
songs and operettas, should have written, as Sullivan
did, the most remarkable oratorio of modern times. To
speak of him, with his great heart in private life, his
adoration of his father and mother, the help he is
always ready to lend to his pupils, and the good he
does without letting anybody know, is the privilege of
a friend, who knows that Sir Arthur Sullivan deserves
as much to be respected as admired.

Yours sincerely
W Barnaby.

Joseph Barnby.

SEVERAL names will be found in this book of famous artists who have shown their great qualifications as children, but if they have proved admirable pupils, there is not one who at the tender age of ten has been a teacher of music. Born in York, in the year 1838, Joseph Barnby, the youngest of seven sons, showed like all his brothers great aptitude for music; but while the others are all acceptable musicians, he showed his powers of execution at the age of seven, when he entered the choir of York Minster, and at the age of ten he had already given such proof of his musical cleverness that he was appointed to teach the other boys. When I say that at twelve he was appointed organist, it will easily be understood that York could not long hold him, and after a few years' exertions in that direction, eager for the fray, he turned his steps towards London, became a student at the Royal Academy of Music, and there competed for the Mendelssohn scholarship. But there he had a hard nut to crack, meeting with a rival competitor a few years his junior, who did secure the prize. Perhaps you have heard his name somewhere. It was Arthur Sullivan. When he was sixteen years old, he was appointed organist at St. Michael's, Queenhithe, then at St. James the Less, Westminster, and finally director of the choir at St. Andrew's,

Wells Street. At that church music was cultivated to such perfection that it established quite a reputation. The great success attained in this way gave Mr. Barnby the idea to start a large choir to do bigger things, and to establish himself as what he must be recognised, viz. one of the best orchestral conductors; for it is well known that if he has succeeded in making his choir by far the best in London, he conducts an orchestra at the same time, and well would it be for many composers if they had the common sense to leave to him what he can do so much better. It has happened quite recently that this excellent choir was found insufficient in a work which, with the best possible performance, would have equally failed. But of course people blamed the choir, not taking into consideration, because they did not know, that the choir had not had a proper rehearsal, either with the solo singers or with the orchestra, and a few hours, so to say, were all that was left them to learn a rather unmusical and in some parts un- vocally written work. Had the conducting been left to Mr. Barnby, he would have taken care to have the proper rehearsals, a proper performance, and would thereby have deprived the composer's friends of an ex- cuse and the choir of a blame which it was not fair under the circumstances to attach to them.

While organist and director at St. Andrew's, Mr. Barnby received a note from an undergraduate at Trinity College, Cambridge, to say that for the vacancy announced at St. Andrew's a young tenor could be re- commended ; would Mr. Barnby travel the short distance and hear him ? Mr. Barnby did, and thought he would risk it, and engaged him on the spot. Whether he did right, and whether his impression guided him correctly, you may judge for yourself when I tell you the name of the young tenor, Edward Lloyd. As to the young undergraduate, he is now the well-known Rector of Sandringham, the Rev. F. A. J. Hervey. Lloyd remained four years studying oratorios with Barnby, who made it a point to go with his choir through the most difficult masses and old oratorios, and to select all the celebrated works of living masters as well. This bore fruit when, in 1870, the Franco-German war drove Gounod to England, and he paid an early visit to St. Andrew's, knowing that there he would hear performed to perfection his 'Messe des Orphéonistes,' 'Vendredi Saint,' 'Les sept dernières paroles,' etc.

When Mr. Barnby conceived the idea to get together a numerous chorus of amateurs, he communicated the idea to several friends, and among others to Sir Julius Benedict, who strongly advised him against it, having himself several times tried and failed. But then Benedict, undoubtedly a clever man and an excellent musician, was a very bad conductor, and lacked the essential quality of organizing and guiding an amateur chorus, a firm will—the very thing that Mr. Barnby possessed in a high degree. Hence it came that where Benedict failed Barnby succeeded. So evident was this at the first concert, that both Benedict and Sims Reeves rushed up to Mr. Barnby to congratulate him on what his skill and his perseverance had achieved. No professional singer is found in that chorus, and what the singers can do they owe to their conductor. The reputation, widespread and well-deserved, of that chorus, has now been so well established that no voice is admitted without a thorough-going severe trial; and thus only is it explained that they send up a volume of tone pure, full, and warm, with which no other chorus can compete. It must however be understood that I always wish to except the Leeds choir so far as the ladies are concerned, because Yorkshire, whence Mr. Barnby comes, has, by a freak of Nature always produced those marvellous voices in the North for which long habit has made us look to the South of Europe.

Meanwhile Mr. Barnby had accepted an engagement to become the musical adviser to the firm of Messrs. Novello & Co., there to carry out the improvement of the cathedral type of music throughout the kingdom. No one in the present day can imagine the shocking state of our cathedral choirs a quarter of a century ago. I call to mind the first service I heard at St. Paul's Cathedral. The choir was represented solely by the boys and *two altos.* No tenor, no basses. One of these two altos evidently considered himself unnecessary, so he remained seated through the entire service, his head enveloped in his surplice, without uttering a sound! Added to this the selection of music performed at that period was of an antiquated character and it may readily be conceived what an effect was produced by the bright services of St. Andrew's, where the finest music was rendered with artistic taste and devotional feeling. By the opportunity he had of introducing the works of new composers (Sullivan, Stainer, Garrett, Tours, etc.) to Messrs. Novello, the ball of modern church music was set rolling. In 1865 Mr. Barnby began the introduction of new or comparatively unknown works, among which such as Bach's 'Two Passions,' 'Christmas Oratorio,' and several cantatas, and Handel's 'Jephtha,' 'Belshazzar's Feast,' 'Theodora,' etc. Beethoven's ' Ninth Symphony' and 'Mass in D' were both performed on the same evening, an unprecedented achievement.

At these concerts was introduced into England the "*diapason normal*," and in Paris a complete set of wind instruments of the required pitch was bought, and an organ built in St. James's Hall to the French pitch. The extraordinary success attending the first few performances of Bach's 'St. Matthew Passion,' with Stockhausen as the Christus, suggested the feasibility of giving this work in church as an integral portion of a Lenten service. And amongst churches what more impressive than Westminster Abbey! But deans and chapters have to be reckoned with ; and who so conservative as these? Nevertheless the scheme laid before Dean Stanley met with no opposition ; nay, even with some encouragement. And in the end this great work was performed, and Westminster Abbey was the scene of the first introduction of the Lenten Passion services which have now become so general.

With this powerful help, Mr. Barnby was now enabled to give a series of concerts, at which he produced grand works by Handel, Bach and others, which had not been heard before in England, at least in this century. He composed an ode for solo, chorus, and orchestra on the occasion of the first visit of the Shah, with Tietjens as the soloist, and he conducted the state performance at the Albert Hall. Also the state performance in the same hall on the occasion of the visit of the Czar to England. He composed an Ode of Welcome, for voices alone, on the first public reception of the Prince of Wales after his return from India; conducted at the state opening of the Fisheries Exhibition, and of the Victoria Hall by her Majesty, the opening of the Colonial Exhibition, also by the Queen, and the second state reception of the Shah a few months ago; and, at the request of the Prince of Wales, he composed the anthem for the wedding of the Duke and Duchess of Fife.

After resigning the position of organist and choir-master at St. Andrew's, Wells Street, Mr. Barnby accepted a similar post at St. Anne's, Soho, where a great feature was made of the weekly performances of Bach's 'St. John Passion' during Lent for thirteen or fourteen years in succession. At these services the Prince and Princess of Wales and the Duke and Duchess of Edinburgh were frequently present. This post he held for fifteen years.

He succeeded Gounod to the conductorship of the Royal Albert Hall Choral Society, with whom he overcame the most complicated difficulties in choral singing with contemporaneous as well as dead masters. It is then evident that besides being an excellent organist and organiser, Mr. Barnby is a most reliable conductor. But there end not his talents, and what he has done as composer is by no means the least valuable jewel in his crown. Having tried his hand in sacred as well as secular music, in songs and in oratorio, and having been

successful in all these directions, it will suffice to point to
'The Lord is King,' which created so favourable an impression at a Leeds Festival, or the oratorio 'Rebekah,'
equally appreciated at the Hereford festival ; and among
songs to 'When the tide comes in,' besides numerous
anthems, motets, hymn tunes, etc., to show that his facile
and sympathetic pen commands profound knowledge,
and can therefore stand the test of every examination.

One of the reasons why the Royal Choral Society is
so efficient, is, that no trouble is spared to get the best
musical material to supply the vacancies which annually
arise on account of death, old age, loss of voice, or
removal from London.   The losses from these and other
causes average about sixty annually.   To supply their
places ten times that number are examined each year.

Mr. Barnby has been appointed precentor and director of musical instruction at Eton.   That he has been
endeavouring to do all the good, able and intelligent instruction could be expected to do them, and that he has
succeeded in this endeavour, is patent from the fact
that not only has he done works of easy dimensions
with his boys, but 'Judas Maccabeus,' Handel's noble
oratorio has been performed, solos, orchestra, and chorus,
all by Eton boys, which proves that as a teacher, as
well as in the career of a composer, he has deserved the
appreciation of a numerous set of distinguished friends.

Mr. Barnby, practical and clever, in private life has
had the good luck to secure a companion both very
attractive and amiable and highly educated, and herself
very clever, which is the most desirable reply to the
rather queer question, "Would you rather marry a pretty

girl or a clever girl?" as if it was a matter of course that all pretty girls must be stupid, or all clever girls plain looking. I offered a friend of mine once some wine, and I said, "Which will you have, sherry or port?" and he answered very solemnly, "Sherry first," which did not exclude port afterwards. Thus Mr. Barnby, to the question above mentioned seems to have answered, "If one quality is good, two must be better," and so he took unto himself a wife both handsome and clever. Mrs. Barnby is a daughter of Lieut.-Col. J. W. Silverthorne, J.P. and Deputy-Lieutenant of the County of Sussex. Two of her brothers hold commissions as captains in the army.

And if a pure conscience, a number of devoted friends, a good wife and handsome children must make a man happy in his public and his private life, then indeed can there be no doubt that Mr. Joseph Barnby is one of the happy men of this world.

1889
E. Albani

Madame Emma Albani-Gye.

MADAME EMMA ALBANI, born in Canada, at Chambly, near Montreal, is of French descent, her maiden name being La Jeunesse—certainly the finest gift, while it lasts, for a vocalist. Canada is rather far away, and it is not very easy to sift the contradictory information given about her father, who, according to one source, was a musical professor and organist of talent, whereas, according to others, he had nothing whatever to do with music. One thing is certain—the little girl possessed a very gifted musical organization. She sang with a purity that attracted attention when she was five or six years old, and, losing her mother at that tender age, she was sent to the Sacré Cœur, a convent in Montreal, where she was taught piano and organ, on both of which instruments she reached a certain degree of proficiency. After several years' study she was sent to New York, where she earned some money as an organist, and when she had saved enough, she left for Paris, the enchanting city, the inhabitants of which are modest enough to say that no artist can have a real reputation who has not received "la consécration de Paris"—*la ville-cerveau*, as Victor Hugo called it. In Paris a few artists received her with prophetic recognition of her future career, and Madame Laffitte, mother of the two greatest beauties under the Empire of Napoleon III., to whom Mdlle. La Jeunesse was specially recommended, took her to Duprez to find out whether the voice she had shown as a child was solid enough to resist the serious study required for a dramatic career. Duprez, whose real artistic effect consisted, above all, in the force of the *tenore robusto*, has put more voices to a severe test—to put it mildly—than any other teacher known. He tried Mdlle. La Jeunesse on the little stage attached to his so-called Conservatoire, and as he found her voice and her health rather delicate, he advised her, after a few months' study, to go to Italy, in the interest both of her health and her study. There she was placed under Signor Lamperti, the father, who, notwithstanding his great age, perhaps on account of it, knew all the traditions of the great singers, past and present, and kept Madame Albani to very hard study of the elements of her art—a precaution as necessary as the solidity of the foundations on which a house is built. She left him after nine months—too early, as soon will be seen,—and made her *début* at Messina, with such effect, that a visit which she received during the evening resulted in an engagement for Malta. But although she succeeded in those two towns, yet, when she arrived highly recommended in London, and sang before Mr. Gye, the father, he, too long-sighted to spoil an *étoile* by producing her too early, sent her back to Italy to renew and continue her studies.

Mr. Gye wanted her then very badly, on account of the tyranny exerted over him by two other *prima donnas*, one of whom he had tried in vain to play against the other. The fact is, he had engaged for next to nothing the most successful *prima donna* of the century. He had another *prima donna*, the greatest actress among all known singers, with the warmest and most sympathetic voice ever heard. But although the first of the two stood in both qualities mentioned not so high as the second, she " drew " better. And here I beg to say a word on this seeming paradox. There are singers, both men and women, who exercise a certain charm over the public, sometimes by their voice and their merits, sometimes for other reasons, called a magnetic attraction, which, in plain English, means an unexplained reason. If this attractive power proves sufficient to bring a large audience every time that singer is announced, the manager can afford to pay a high salary, sure to be repaid by the public. But, on the other hand, the study, talent, and merit of a singer may reach up to any height, yet if the public are not anxious to be present, the money does not come in, and the manager cannot afford to pay the price which he would be enabled to pay by the certainty of a full house. Thus it is that very meritorious singers often say : " Why should I not be paid as much as So-and-so ? Do I not sing as well ? " Undoubtedly ; but the invisible, the unexplained charm which draws the public in masses to the performance of " So-and-so " is just " So-and-so's " privileged monopoly ! Madame Albani is certainly as great a singer, and in oratorio a much greater singer, than Madame Patti, yet I have seen Madame Patti draw over £1,600 to the Albert Hall on a day in November with the thickest fog of the year from early

morning till night. No other singer known could do
that. See again Mr. Lloyd, in the force of his age and
his talent, who has all the knowledge, tone-production,
and advantage of voice which twenty years' difference of
age give him over Sims Reeves. Yet he is paid about
half his terms. Why? Because in certain concerts
and with certain pieces Sims Reeves is supposed to fill
the hall by himself.

Mr. Gye, then, had engaged a young *prima donna* on
the hardest conditions for a *débutante*, though she was
one of the most successful imaginable. But as her wings
grew, so did her pretensions. He then engaged the other
one above mentioned, who was a real acquisition, only
she wanted the same *rôles* precisely that were given to
her rival.

As No. 1 would not play second fiddle to anybody,
and as the Director wished to play her against the other
one, and, therefore, had courted her to a great extent,
he was not a little astonished when, after seeing her
one afternoon at her house, and having announced her
for the following night, he was at 9.30 in the evening
the recipient of a telegram, dated Calais, and worded
à peu près as follows: "I am a first *prima donna*.
What you seem to want is a seconda donna. That is
no employment for me. I am off. Good-bye." Mr. Gye
having tried the youthful, too youthful, daughter of a
celebrated pianist in vain, he then came back to the
truant who had placed the sea between him and her.
At last he saw that Madame Albani might rise high
enough in merit and talent to sustain the artistic
struggle, and she fulfilled his expectation. In poetical

simplicity as Elsa, in dramatic intensity as Norma, in idyllic charm as Mignon, Madame Albani has great claims to an exceptional artistic position. She has the quality, which mostly captivates the public, of very high notes, but, in my humble opinion, she has laid too much stress upon them ; and although I fully admit that she has a sweetness and an art in producing them, yet there is no concealing the fact that she has strained and, to a certain extent, sacrificed the steadiness of her medium, several notes of which have of late evinced signs of trembling, or at least of unsteadiness, which ought to be a warning to the great *prima donna*. At the same time, she is just in the age where mediums grow fullest, being at least ten years younger than Madame Patti ; and if she will listen to good and friendly advice, she will not lay so much weight upon those high notes, so that she may keep her voice in its full power for a long time to come, and delight her friends and admirers as a concert, oratorio, and dramatic singer rarely equalled.

Her house is filled with works of art, both paintings and sculpture. She is as tender a mother as she is a wife, and she attends to her home duties and to her embroidery needle as any German lady would. Perhaps it is owing to these qualities, combined with her great artistic talent, that she owes the marked preference which the Queen has, on so many occasions, shown her, sometimes in quite exceptional ways, not only by costly and tasteful jewellery, but for instance by such gifts as "More Leaves from my Journal in the Highlands," on the fly-sheet of which the Queen has written with her own hand : " To Madame Albani-Gye, with warm thanks

for the great pleasure of hearing her sing, from Victoria
R.I., Balmoral, September 24, 1885." While Madame
Albani was singing in Berlin, at the Imperial Palace,
Count Seckendorf put into her hands a telegram, which
the Queen had sent to her daughter, then Crown
Princess, recommending Madame Albani as "her
Canadian subject, in whom she takes great interest."
A *tour de force* which Madame Albani accomplished,
and which is not always successfully tried by other
prime donne, is that she sang once, in St. Petersburg,
a song in Russian, without understanding a word of it,
yet pronouncing it so as to drive the audience frantic.

Madame Albani married in 1878, Mr. Ernest Gye,
and her little son, her only child, is now nine years old.
The whole treasure of tenderness in a young mother's
heart, you will easily discover in Madame Albani, if
you look at the picture of the heir-apparent, and hear
her say in an accent which no music can render : "This
is my son." The look which accompanies this statement implies : What do you think of this masterpiece
of creation ?

Madame Albani has distinctions, triumphs, testi-
monials, laurels, and presents and medals in profusion.
She received the Jubilee medal of the Emperor William
(given to her by the revered old monarch in February,
1886, when she sang a season at the Royal Opera in
Berlin). She was appointed Kammersängerinn to the
German Court, when, at her first visit to Berlin, she
sang Elsa in 'Lohengrin,' in German, beside her usual
répertoire. In the next year, 1887, Madame Albani
received from her Majesty the much-coveted Jubilee

Order medal, together with a diamond and sapphire crown brooch, which the Queen gave her in Balmoral. The order of merit and the medal of the King of Denmark she received from the King, at the Royal Palace in Copenhagen, in 1887. These two distinctions were "sandwiched" by King Kalakua's order and cross. The great facility with which Madame Albani, French by birth, sings English, Italian, French, and even German, has excited the admiration of hundreds of journalists. The French grace of her build, her elegant toilettes, and her earnest study of mimical accomplishments, have made her famous in the annals of her time, so that one of the greatest attractions on the platform is Madame Emma Albani-Gye.

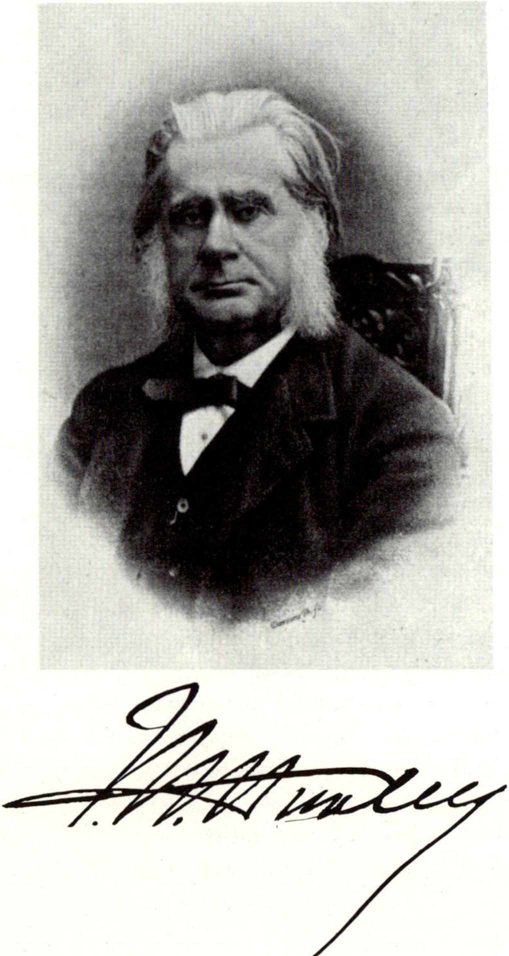

Professor Huxley.

THE following letter of Professor Huxley, in its simple grace and eloquence needs no commentary, it speaks for itself.—L. E.

"MY DEAR MR. ENGEL,—

"You really are the most pertinaciously persuasive of men. When you first wrote to me, I said I would have nothing whatever to do with anything you might please to say about me, that I had a profound objection to write about myself, and that I could not see what business the public had with my private life. I think I even expressed to you my complete sympathy with Dr. Johnson's desire to take Boswell's life when he heard of the latter's occupation with his biography.

"Undeterred by all this, you put before me the alternative of issuing something that may be all wrong, unless I furnish you with something authoritative; I do not say all right, because autobiographies are essentially works of fiction, whatever biographies may be. So I yield, and send you what follows, in the hope that those who find it to be mere egotistical gossip will blame you and not me.

"I am,

"Yours faithfully,

"T. H. HUXLEY."

I was born about eight o'clock in the morning on the 4th of May, 1825, at Ealing, which was, at that time, as quiet a little country village as could be found within half a dozen miles of Hyde Park Corner. Now it is a suburb of London with, I believe, 30,000 inhabitants. I am not aware that any portents preceded my arrival in this world; but, in my childhood, I remember hearing a traditional account of the manner in which I lost the chance of an endowment of great practical value. The windows of my mother's room were open, in consequence of the unusual warmth of the weather. For the same reason, probably, a neighbouring bee-hive had swarmed, and the new colony, pitching on the window-sill, was making its way into the room when the horrified nurse shut down the sash. If that well-meaning woman had only abstained from her ill-timed interference, the swarm might have settled on my lips, and I should have been endowed with that mellifluous eloquence which, in this country, leads far more surely than worth, capacity, or honest work, to the highest places in Church and State. But the opportunity was lost, and I have been obliged to content myself through life with saying what I mean in the plainest of plain language ; than which, I suppose, there is no habit more ruinous to a man's prospects of advancement. Why I was christened Thomas Henry I do not know ; but it is a curious chance that my parents should have fixed for my usual denomination upon the name of that particular Apostle with whom I have always felt most sympathy. Physically and mentally I am the son of my mother so completely—even down to peculiar movements of the hands, which made their appearance in me as I reached the age she had when I noticed them—that I can hardly find any trace of my father in myself, except an inborn faculty for drawing, which unfortunately, in my case, has never been cultivated ; a hot temper ; and that amount of tenacity of purpose, which unfriendly observers sometimes call obstinacy.

My mother was a slender brunette, of an emotional

and energetic temperament, and possessed of the most piercing black eyes I ever saw in a woman's head. With no more education than other women of the middle classes in her day, she had an excellent mental capacity. Her most distinguishing characteristic, however, was rapidity of thought. If one ventured to suggest that she had not taken much time to arrive at any conclusion, she would say, "I cannot help it, things flash across me." That peculiarity has been passed on to me in full strength; it has often stood me in good stead; it has sometimes played me sad tricks, and it has always been a danger. But after all, if my time were to come over again, there is nothing I would less willingly part with than my inheritance of mother wit.

I have next to nothing to say about my childhood. In later years, my mother, looking at me almost reproachfully, would sometimes say, "Ah! you were such a pretty boy!" whence I had no difficulty in concluding that I had not fulfilled my early promise in the matter of looks. In fact, I have a distinct recollection of certain curls, of which I was vain, and of a conviction that I closely resembled that handsome courtly gentleman, Sir Herbert Oakley, who was vicar of our parish, and who was as a god to us country folk, because he was occasionally visited by the then Prince George of Cambridge. I remember turning my pinafore wrong side forwards, in order to represent a surplice, and preaching to my mother's maids in the kitchen, as nearly as possible in Sir Herbert's manner, one Sunday morning when the rest of the family were at church. That is the earliest indication I can call to mind of the strong clerical affinities which my friend Mr. Herbert Spencer has always ascribed to me, though I fancy they have for the most part remained in a latent state.

My regular school training was of the briefest, perhaps fortunately, for though my way of life has made me acquainted with all sorts and conditions of men, from the highest to the lowest, I deliberately affirm that the society I fell into at school was the worst I have ever known. We boys were average lads, with much the same inherent capacity for good and evil as any others ; but the people who were set over us cared about as much for our intellectual and moral welfare as if they were baby farmers. We were left to the operation of the struggle for existence among ourselves, and bullying was the least of the ill practices current among us. Almost the only cheerful reminiscence in connection with the place, which arises in my mind, is that of a battle I had with one of my classmates, who had bullied me until I could stand it no longer. I was a very slight lad, but there was a wild-cat element in me which, when roused, made up for lack of weight, and I licked my adversary effectually. However, one of my first experiences of the extremely rough-and-ready nature of Justice, as exhibited by the course of things in general, arose out of the fact that I, the victor, had a black eye, while he, the vanquished, had none ; so that I got into disgrace, and he did not. We made it up, and thereafter I was unmolested. One of the greatest shocks I ever received in my life was to be told, a dozen years afterwards, by the groom who brought me my horse, in a stable-yard in Sydney, that he was my quondam antagonist. He had a long story of family misfortune to account for his position ; but at that time it was necessary to deal very cautiously with mysterious strangers in New South Wales, and on inquiry I found that the unfortunate young man had not only been " sent out," but had undergone more than one colonial conviction.

As I grew older, my great desire was to be a mechanical engineer, but the Fates were against this ; and, while very young, I commenced the study of Medicine under a medical brother-in-law. But, though the Institute of Mechanical Engineers would certainly not own me, I am not sure that I have not, all along, been a sort of mechanical engineer *in partibus infidelium.* I am now occasionally horrified to think how very little I ever knew or cared about Medicine as the art of healing. The only part of my professional course which really and deeply interested me was Physiology, which is the mechanical engineering of living machines ; and, notwithstanding that natural science has been my proper business, I am afraid there is very little of the genuine naturalist in me. I never collected anything, and species work was always a burden to me ; what I cared for was the architectural and engineering part of the business, the working out the wonderful unity of plan in the thousands and thousands of diverse living constructions, and the modifications of similar apparatuses to serve diverse ends. The extraordinary attraction I felt towards the study of the intricacies of living structure nearly proved fatal to me at the outset. I was a mere boy—I think between thirteen and fourteen years of age—when I was taken by some older student friends of mine to the first post-mortem examination I ever attended. All my life I have been most unfortunately sensitive to the disagreeables which attend anatomical pursuits ; but on this occasion, my curiosity overpowered all other feelings, and I spent two or three hours in gratifying it. I did not cut myself, and none of the ordinary symptoms of dissection poison supervened, but poisoned I was some- how, and I remember sinking into a strange state of apathy. By way of a last chance I was sent to the care of some good, kind people, friends of my father's, who lived in a farmhouse in the heart of Warwickshire. I remember staggering from my bed to the window on the bright spring morning after my arrival, and throwing open the casement. Life seemed to come back on the wings of the breeze ; and, to this day, the faint odour of wood-smoke, like that which floated across the farm- yard in the early morning, is as good to me as the "sweet south upon a bed of violets." I soon recovered ; but for years I suffered from occasional paroxysms of internal pain, and from that time my constant friend, hypochondriacal dyspepsia, commenced his half century of co-tenancy of my fleshly tabernacle.

Looking back on my " Lehrjahre," I am sorry to say that I do not think that any account of my doings as a student would tend to edification. In fact, I should distinctly warn ingenuous youth to avoid imitating my example. I worked extremely hard when it pleased me, and when it did not (which was a very frequent case) I was extremely idle (unless making caricatures of one's pastors and masters is to be called a branch of in- dustry), or else wasted my energies in wrong directions.

I read everything I could lay hands upon, including novels, and took up all sorts of pursuits, to drop them again quite as speedily. No doubt it was very largely my own fault, but the only instruction from which I ever obtained the proper effect of education was that which I received from Mr. Wharton Jones, who was the Lecturer on Physiology at the Charing Cross School of Medicine. The extent and precision of his knowledge impressed me greatly, and the severe exactness of his method of lecturing was quite to my taste. I do not know that I have ever felt so much respect for anybody before or since. I worked hard to obtain his approbation, and he was extremely kind and helpful to the youngster who, I am afraid, took up more of his time than he had any right to do. It was he who suggested the publication of my first scientific paper—a very little one—in the *Medical Gazette* of 1845, and most kindly corrected the literary faults which abounded in it, short as it was; for at that time, and for many years afterwards, I detested the trouble of writing, and would take no pains over it.

It was in the early spring of 1846 that, having finished my obligatory medical studies, and passed the first M.B. examination at the London University (though I was still too young to qualify at the College of Surgeons), I was talking to a fellow-student—the present eminent physician, Sir Joseph Fayrer—and wondering what I should do to meet the imperative necessity for earning my own bread, when my friend suggested that I should write to Sir William Burnett, at that time Director-General for the Medical Service of the Navy, for an appointment. I thought this rather a strong thing to do, as Sir William was personally unknown to me, but my cheery friend would not listen to my scruples, so I went to my lodgings and wrote the best letter I could devise. A few days afterwards I received the usual official circular of acknowledgment, but at the bottom there was written an instruction to call at Somerset House on such a day. I thought that looked like business, so, at the appointed time, I called and sent in my card, while I waited in Sir William's ante-room. He was a tall, shrewd-looking old gentleman, with a broad Scotch accent—and I think I see him now as he entered with my card in his hand. The first thing he did was to return it, with the frugal reminder that I should probably find it useful on some other occasion. The second was to ask whether I was an Irishman. I suppose the air of modesty about my appeal must have struck him. I satisfied the Director-General that I was English to the backbone, and he made some inquiries as to my student career, finally desiring me to hold myself ready for examination. Having passed this, I was in Her Majesty's Service, and entered on the books of Nelson's old ship *Victory*, for duty at Haslar Hospital, about a couple of months after I made my application.

My official chief at Haslar was a very remarkable person—the late Sir John Richardson, an excellent naturalist, and far-famed as an indomitable Arctic traveller. He was a silent, reserved man outside the circle of his family and intimates; and, having a full share of youthful vanity, I was extremely disgusted to find that "Old John," as we irreverent youngsters called him, took not the slightest notice of my worshipful self, either the first time I attended him, as it was my duty to do, or for some weeks afterwards. I am afraid to think of the lengths to which my tongue might have run on the subject of the churlishness of the chief, who was in truth one of the kindest-hearted and most considerate of men. But one day, as I was crossing the Hospital square, Sir John stopped me, and heaped coals of fire on my head by telling me that he had tried to get me one of the resident appointments, much coveted by the assistant-surgeons, but that the Admiralty had put in another man. "However," said he, "I mean to keep you here till I can get you something you will like," and turned upon his heel without waiting for the thanks I stammered out. That explained how it was I had not been packed off to the West Coast of Africa, like some of my juniors, and why, eventually, I remained alto-gether seven months at Haslar.

After a long interval, during which "Old John" ignored my existence almost as completely as before, he stopped me again as we met in a casual way, and describing the service on which the *Rattlesnake* was likely to be employed, said that Captain Owen Stanley, who was to command the ship, had asked him to recommend an assistant-surgeon who knew something of science ; would I like that ? Of course I jumped at the offer. "Very well, I give you leave ; go to London at once and see Captain Stanley." I went, saw my future commander, who was very civil to me and promised to ask that I should be appointed to his ship, as in due time I was. It is a singular thing that, during the few

K

months of my stay at Haslar, I had among my mess-
mates two future Directors-General of the Medical
Service of the Navy (Sir Alexander Armstrong and Sir
John Watt-Reid), with the present President of the
College of Physicians and my kindest of doctors, Sir
Andrew Clark.   Life on board Her Majesty's ships in
those days was a very different affair from what it is
now ; and ours was exceptionally rough, as we were
often many months without receiving letters or seeing
any civilized people but ourselves.   In exchange, we had
the interest of being about the last voyagers, I suppose,
to whom it could be possible to meet with people who
knew nothing of fire-arms—as we did on the South
Coast of New Guinea—and of making acquaintance with
a variety of interesting savage and semi-civilised people.
But, apart from experience of this kind, and the opportunities offered for scientific work, to me, personally, the
cruise was extremely valuable.   It was good for me to
live under sharp discipline ; to be down on the realities
of existence by living on bare necessaries ; to find out
how extremely well worth living life seemed to be, when
one woke up from a night's rest on a soft plank, with
the sky for canopy and cocoa and weevilly biscuit the
sole prospect for breakfast ; and more especially to learn
to work for the sake of what I got for myself out of it,
even if it all went to the bottom and I along with it.
My brother officers were as good fellows as sailors ought
to be and generally are ; but, naturally, they neither
knew nor cared anything about my pursuits, nor understood why I should be so zealous in pursuit of the
objects which my friends the Middies christened "Buf-

fons," after the title conspicuous on a volume of the "Suites à Buffon," which stood on my shelf in the chart room.

During the four years of our absence, I sent home communication after communication to the "Linnean Society," with the same result as that obtained by Noah when he sent the raven out of his ark. Tired at last of hearing nothing about them, I determined to do or die, and, in 1849, I drew up a more elaborate paper and forwarded it to the Royal Society. This was my dove, if I had only known it. But owing to the movements of the ship, I heard nothing of that either, until my return to England in the latter end of the year 1850, when I found that it was printed and published, and that a huge packet of separate copies awaited me. When I hear some of my young friends complain of want of sympathy and encouragement, I am inclined to think that my naval life was not the least valuable part of my education.

Three years after my return were occupied by a battle between my scientific friends on the one hand, and the Admiralty on the other, as to whether the latter ought, or ought not, to act up to the spirit of a pledge they had given to encourage officers who had done scientific work, by contributing to the expense of publishing mine. At last the Admiralty, getting tired, I suppose, cut short the discussion by ordering me to join a ship. Which thing I declined to do, and as Rastignac, in the Père Goriot, says to Paris, I said to London, "*à nous deux.*" I desired to obtain a Professorship of either Physiology or Comparative Anatomy ; and as vacancies

occurred, I applied, but in vain.   My friend, Professor
Tyndall, and I were candidates at the same time, he for
the Chair of Physics and I for that of Natural History,
in the University of Toronto, which fortunately, as it
turned out, would not look at either of us.   I say fortunately, not from any lack of respect for Toronto, but
because I soon made up my mind that London was the
place for me, and hence I have steadily declined the in-
ducements to leave it which have at various times been
offered.   At last, in 1854, on the translation of my
warm friend, Edward Forbes, to Edinburgh, Sir Henry
De la Beche, the Director-General of the Geological
Survey, offered me the post Forbes vacated of Paleonto-
logist and Lecturer on Natural History.   I refused the
former point blank, and accepted the latter provisionally,
telling Sir Henry that I did not care for fossils, and that
I should give up Natural History as soon as I could get
a physiological post.   But I held the office for thirty-one
years, and a large part of my work has been paleonto-
logical.

At that time I disliked public speaking, and had a
firm conviction that I should break down every time I
opened my mouth.   I believe I had every fault a speaker
could have (except talking at random or indulging in
rhetoric) when I spoke to the first important audience I
ever addressed, on a Friday evening, at the Royal Institution, in 1852.   Yet I must confess to having been
guilty, *malgré moi*, of as much public speaking as most
of my contemporaries, and for the last ten years it
ceased to be so much of a bugbear to me.   I used to
pity myself for having to go through this training ; but

I am now more disposed to compassionate the unfortunate audiences, especially my ever friendly hearers at the Royal Institution, who were the subjects of my oratorical experiments.

The last thing that it would be proper for me to do would be to speak of the work of my life, or to say at the end of the day, whether I think I have earned my wages or not. Men are said to be partial judges of themselves—young men may be, I doubt if old men are. Life seems terribly foreshortened as they look back ; and the mountain they set themselves to climb in youth turns out to be a mere spur of immeasurably higher ranges, when, with failing breath, they reach the top. But if I may speak of the objects I have had more or less definitely in view since I began the ascent of my hillock, they are briefly these : to promote the increase of natural knowledge and to forward the application of scientific methods of investigation to all the problems of life to the best of my ability, in the conviction—which has grown with my growth and strengthened with my strength—that there is no alleviation for the sufferings of mankind except veracity of thought and of action, and the resolute facing of the world as it is, when the garment of makebelieve, by which pious hands have hidden its uglier features, is stripped off.

It is with this intent that I have subordinated any reasonable or unreasonable ambition for scientific fame, which I may have permitted myself to entertain, to other ends ; to the popularization of science ; to the development and organization of scientific education ; to the endless series of battles and skirmishes over evolution ; and to untiring opposition to that ecclesiastical spirit, that clericalism, which in England, as everywhere else, and to whatever denomination it may belong, is the deadly enemy of science.

In striving for the attainment of these objects, I have been but one among many, and I shall be well content to be remembered, or even not remembered, as such. Circumstances, among which I am proud to reckon the devoted kindness of many friends, have led to my occupation of various prominent positions, among which the Presidency of the Royal Society is the highest. It would be mock modesty on my part, with these and other scientific honours which have been bestowed upon me, to pretend that I have not succeeded in the career which I have followed, rather because I was driven into it, than of my own free will; but I am afraid I should not count even these things as marks of success, if I could not hope that I had somewhat helped that movement of opinion which has been called the New Reformation.

Hubert Herkomer.

'MY DEAR FRIEND,—

"But for you I would never have written this story of my life, and my children and I will ever be thankful to you for having made me do it.

"*Ever yours,*

"*HUBERT HERKOMER.*"

WE are all Bavarians; and my father's family belong to Waal, a small village of a thousand inhabitants near Landsberg am Lech.

My father's earliest recollections are of having to visit his grandparents from time to time at a neighbouring village, when the whole day seemed to be spent in prayer; for the old people—his grandparents—were still direct sufferers from the Thirty Years War.

My grandfather was by trade a mason; by nature an inventor of the first order. His chances in life for the display of this faculty were small indeed; and when he left his trade to take charge of the little house and field property, his chances were smaller still. (I should explain that his mother had the right to keep back one son from military service, and chose him, as his brothers were all drunkards and gamblers. Their example filled him with a horror of these vices which he impressed on my father; who, in his turn, never touched a card even for harmless play.)

But here he did marvels in the way of locks for gates and cupboards, and in all manner of mechanical contrivances for use or curiosity. I take him as my starting-point, since he probably originated in our family the feeling for the kind of life that my father struggled after and which it fell to my blessed lot to enjoy—the artist's life.

The earliest picture in our family history is a grim one. It is the picture, brought vividly to my mind by description, of my grandfather tending horses through the night in the open, when he was about ten or twelve years old. The night would not be grim but for the peculiar neigh of the horses, proving the presence of a stench that comes only from dead bodies: and there they hang—human beings, dangling from a gibbet on this side and on that. Fear was not in the boy; but these ghastly companions through the night made him think. And as he gazed at the stars, he learned, untaught, to tell the hour of the night.

This boy invented a method of carrying down the horses' food from the loft to the manger by divided channels, an arrangement that is now considered indispensable. At the time people wondered when they saw it, and asked who made it. The answer was, "Our boy."

On one occasion, during his apprenticeship to his trade of mason, he was sent with a message to a silver-smith. Whilst the silversmith was absent on the business of the message, the boy saw lying near him the chain that was in making. Without more ado he began working at it, and by the time the other returned, had completed an inch of chain, of workmanship equal to the master's.

My grandfather was nearly thirty when he learned to

read and write. I possess a prize which he gained at the Feiertags-Schule, a book full of useful hints, moral and mechanical. The newly-gained power of reading naturally had a great effect upon such a mind; and he was the first in all the neighbourhood to buy books, which he did when once he came to his "Heimath Gut." He worked on the imaginations, such as they were, of the peasants, and induced them to join in putting aside money with him for the purchase of books, to be read by all in turn. Perhaps only three were bought in a year, but they were read, and appreciated too. In this atmosphere it was that my father got his love of reading, which he kept until within a month of his death.

My grandfather—a man of real genius—was blessed with an excellent wife, strong in body and eminently sensible in mind, by whom he had four sons and two daughters, all strong and healthy children. This good woman was selected by the community to study mid-wifery at the public expense, which she did for some months at a hospital at Munich, called, I think, the "Frauen Institut."

The grandfather made all his four boys use tools, and they produced those quaint groups so familiar in German country churches, a favourite subject being the Nativity. In these *relief-pictures* the hands, feet, and faces are carved in wood and painted: the draperies are of real stuff, dipped in glue and allowed to stiffen in the folds desired, and afterwards painted, with gilt borders added, and so forth.

When my father was four years old, a famine, only less severe than that in the last century, visited many parts of Germany, and in the families around there was terrible distress ; but his mother wisely gave her children oatmeal, which was obtainable but considered food unfit for human beings. In this way she saved them, but she wept as she saw them devouring it.

This trouble past, one is inclined to linger on that type of home, so essentially German—a house to live in, a garden, and land enough to yield food for the family should no disaster occur—and all this one's own property ; a craftsman, with time in the intervals of his modest field-work for many little improvements, with a wise and good wife and healthy children around him ; free from all debt and anxiety as to means ; with a God and a Church he believes in, and time to think and reflect,—surely here is a picture not easily surpassed of man's wants supplied. But I believe it needs the German character to gild such a life with the purifying influence of an ideal, without which every life becomes a mere existence. Take the English or French peasant under similar circumstances, and you will find little striving after an ideal when the conditions of life imposed upon them remain the same from year to year. The life I speak of did not fail of its effect upon the children, who were destined to have such various experiences in life, so far removed from that small " Heimath."

The question of apprenticing the boys now had to be faced. The eldest son was put with a barber, as a preparatory step to his becoming a doctor, a universal practice in Germany in those days. The country doctor did all the shaving as well as the more serious work ;

the ordinary blood-letting—so fashionable then—being usually left to the assistant or apprentice.

My father, the second son, was apprenticed to a joiner, or "Tischler," the third son to a weaver, and the fourth to a turner. All four turned out exceptionally clever. The youngest died of a fever while still a boy, but my father always spoke of him as by far the cleverest of them all.

" *Sei ehrlich und fleissig,*"—Be honest and industrious, —were the words with which my grandfather left my father at his new master's, in Munich. His apprentice-ship there is an interesting picture : the boy, with no instruction in his trade except such as he picked up for himself, doing menial work for the master—cleaning his boots, and the like, sitting at the same table with the family, although scarcely ever getting quite enough to eat —and very little was the money he received from home ; taken on Sundays, with all the other apprentices of the various trades, to the three schools—the day school, the Sunday school, and the drawing school.

It was the last of these that fascinated him, and he worked hard to compete for the medal given for the best drawing. His means, however, quite prevented his buying the right materials for it, until the master, Hanf-staengl (father of the present successful photographer in Munich), seeing how full of promise the boy was, gave him what was necessary. The result was a triumph. A medal was presented to him by the mayor in the great town hall, with true Nüremberger pomp and ceremony—the only time, my father often said, when he never felt his legs !

Nowadays all this is gone, there are only nominal apprentices, and they are not escorted to the different schools on Sundays, as in those times, by a body-guard of policemen. Nor has the apprentice now any chance of distinctions until he emerges into the journeyman workman. "The journeyman workman," I do not know the origin of the term, but it is peculiarly applicable to the custom of those times. The "Handwerksbursch" was the young craftsman who had passed from the apprentice into the workman, and then wandered on foot from place to place, from country to country, gaining experience, until he felt able to make his "masterpiece"; after which, and not before, he was permitted to establish himself in business and call himself *master*. My father's wanderings on foot took him to Amsterdam, and back by way of Paris to Munich, and they were among the most delightful experiences of his life.

It was said that his "masterpiece" was much better than was needed to enable him to pass.

When my grandfather died my father took over the small property and established himself in Waal as a "Tischler Meister"; when the first thing he did was to pull down the old house, and build a new one to his taste. Simple as this was, it was original and different from the others in the village, calling forth the familiar remark that "those Herkomers never did anything like other people"—a remark, by the way, that people have been good enough to make about me in the third generation. So strong was local feeling, indeed, that to soothe it my father took down a little turret which he had built on the front of the house, and which, as the house is still standing and in good hands, I hope some day to restore.

Orders for work came in fast to the young " Meister." Among others, the altar in the church needed not only restoring, but enlarging; an undertaking to which he was quite equal, thanks to the work he had done in his leisure hours. For besides working at geometry and perspective, he had made a thorough study of Gothic style. Apart from his scientific knowledge, he was an excellent draughtsman, as is shown in those remarkable drawings for which he obtained the medal, and which, I rejoice to say, are now at Bushey.

Soon came the marriage of Lorenz Herkomer, master-joiner, to Josephine Niggl, spinster, as the parish register records. Her father was schoolmaster in a neighbouring village, one of a class who at that time in Germany held a position next in importance to that of the parish priest. The schoolmaster was always something of a musician too, for he had to provide the music in church, and every child was taught to play upon some instrument. Indeed, very many good musicians have been schoolmasters first, or have been the sons of schoolmasters. And so it happened that all my mother's family were musical, and she herself could play the violin as well as the piano. Of the rest, a son of one of her sisters is now schoolmaster at Oberammergau, having been specially chosen for his musical ability to improve the music at the Passion Play; another nephew of hers, a priest who died young, was well known in his part of the country for his superb tenor voice; and two daughters of another sister, Marie and

Mathilde Wurm, are both known in the musical world, the former of them having gained a Mendelssohn scholarship at London. The father of these last, by the way, was a typical German schoolmaster, who, however, came over to England, and has now lived for many years as a teacher of music at Southampton, where all his children were born.

My father's marriage was a most happy one. Large and strong as his nature was, it was wonderfully tender also, and his devotion to my mother, with her sensitive and spiritual organization, was quite ideal.

I was born in 1849, and was their only child. When I came into the world, my father was heard to say, " This boy shall be my best friend, and he shall be a painter ; " and I remember very well, when this was afterwards told me as a boy, the solemn and impressive feeling which the words left with me, and which I never lost. Those who saw my father in his last years, at Bushey, will know that I was privileged to fulfil the first part of this prediction.

For two years after this my parents remained at Waal ; at the end of which time they decided to emigrate to America. The reasons which led them to this step were, partly the narrow restrictions and limitations of a village-life in matters political and religious—even in a self-supporting village such as ours was—which to a man of my father's spirit were extremely irksome, and partly the unsettled state of the country. For Germany was still trembling from the effects of the year '48. Laws were changed at the demand of the people, but though they gained their objects, their leaders, strong and patriotic men, were banished or imprisoned, unless they fled to America ; which was not considered a very reputable thing to do, as it was generally held to denote a desire to escape the gallows. My father himself took no active part in the revolution, though on some points his ardent nature felt very keenly and strongly. His youngest brother, John, had served six years in the army, having drawn a low number in the conscription, whereas my father had drawn a high number, and so was exempt from military duty. The last year of my uncle's term of service carried him through '48, but he never came into direct contact with the rebels. On the whole he enjoyed his military life. He was well known in his regiment for his excellent pen-and-ink portraits, which were in great request among the officers. At the time I speak of he had already gone to America, and thither my parents also now decided to go.

America was the new craze then—a very land of promise. And so the " Heimath-Gut " was sold, to supply the money for the journey ; and with stout heart my father started, a manly and able craftsman, with wife and two-year-old baby, for the new world.

Emigrants now who make the passage in some of the largest and fastest steamers that cross the Atlantic, little know what their predecessors at that time had to endure in those horrible sailing vessels. The passage took six weeks, with salt meat for food, and only a scanty supply of water. Neither my mother nor I would have survived the voyage, I have been told, but for a happy forethought of my father's, who before starting had condensed some milk to take with us. This, eked out by what little water we got, kept us both alive. We were a shade better off than my uncle, though, for in the vessel in which he had crossed, there was but one stove, upon which the whole number of emigrants had to cook their own food. The misery of it can be imagined.

The arrival in New York opened out the usual channels for rascality, intimidation, and theft. There were no Castle Gardens then to protect the new arrivals, with licensed lodging-house keepers to take them up. The circular building known by that name, which is now used for the reception and protection of emigrants, situated at the very end of New York, was then a concert hall in the fashionable part of the town, and was in fact the hall in which Jennie Lind made her *debût* under Barnum's clever management. (I say *clever*, because he threw himself upon the moral side of the character of a nation which had so singular a prejudice against all public singers ; and with this peerless lady he triumphed.)

My parents stayed a year or so in New York, and then moved to Rochester, and finally to Cleveland, Ohio, always in company with my uncle John. My other uncle, the weaver, had also come over, but he never resided with us. He still lives in America, at Long Island, a strong hale man of more than seventy, who for the last five years has been working entirely for me.

The German emigrants of those days were not looked upon with much favour by the Americans (to whom, by the way, they were all " Dutch "), any more than were the Irish, for that matter, both being equally held up to opprobrium. As a natural consequence, there was little sympathy between the races on any point. The Germans fought for their German Sunday, as they knew it at home, and could find no reason for the puritanical Sabbath of the Americans. Endless trouble arose from stealthy drinking in the beerhouses which Germans had established, with their own beer, for their countrymen. The whole character of the one nation contrasted curiously with that of the other; the cool, practical nature of the American on the one hand, and on the other the German temperament, with its heated and vague revolutionary outbursts. The politics of both countries were the subject of vehement discussion, and of course religion came in for its share—through it all running a strange desire to pull everything to pieces.

For such a character as my father's, this life was a crisis—one through which, fortunately, he passed safely.

The work done in America was not artistic, and it was the absence of artistic and romantic elements in the new country which made the trial all the more bitter to him and my uncle John, and perhaps prejudiced them unduly against the Americans. The Teutonic feeling for the romantic in nature was strong in my father, and his rambles through every available wood or forest—longing as he was for some touch of the old home picturesqueness —were invariably spoilt by the presence of dead cattle, bits of old iron, or some equally sordid refuse. When once the love of a German pine forest has entered into the soul of a German, he cannot do without a sight of it for long at a time,—a feeling that I know myself,

L

although I was sixteen before I saw a real German
"Tannenwald." But nothing of this, nothing of the
romance, both musical and pictorial, that surrounds the
German hunter's life—the "Jägerleben"—could find any
echo among the loafers who shot any and every animal
that ran and every bird that flew within their reach.
There was no use in looking there for the deer that one
might see anywhere springing through the German forest.
Everything there seemed to be done to *abuse* nature.

After the absence of romance, the lack of architectural style or any taste for art seemed the hardest thing
to bear.   Now and again a picture would come from
Europe on show, and they felt a hungry desire to see it:
Duboeuf's 'Adam and Eve' was one they particularly
liked and remembered.   So these artists had to carve
great figures for figureheads to ships, big wooden
brackets for houses (to be afterwards covered with sand,
to make them look *stony*), and anything and everything
except the noble work they were capable of doing.
Their recreation was painting, chiefly in the way of experiment with grounds and colours; for it was a fancy
of theirs that the secret of fine colouring lay in the
choice of the ground upon which to paint, or in some
peculiar method of underpainting.   In this way hundreds and hundreds of little heads were painted, of
course not from nature, in order to test certain experiments in grounds, to be afterwards exposed to light and
air for so many months.

Sometimes a stray portrait would be ordered; and
this would be painted from a photograph.   One portrait
of an elderly man provoked the inquiry, " Where's the

old gentleman's smile?" Another, of a little child, was successful owing to the introduction of the little "cunning" foot.

In Cleveland my mother began to give lessons in music, with great distress of mind, as she could not speak the language; but it was not long before she learned enough to make herself understood, and her pupils soon came to appreciate and love her. It was at her pupils' concerts that I first appeared in public in a musical capacity. I have been told that I could sing any simple tune that I heard when four years old, but never *would* sing unless a guitar were put in my hands —which, of course, I could not play. It must have been the desire of producing the best effect, even then.

From my fourth to my eighth year I was possessed by various crazes; for months I would make nothing but mechanical clowns, that jumped when one pulled a string; at another time it would be all toy waggons and carts; and I have often been told since that however rudely they were made—with buttons and pins,—they always worked well, and would "go." That I already had a leaning to musical expression is brought to my mind by a little incident that I still well remember. With Germans the Christmas tree is supposed to be brought by Santa Claus, secretly. One Christmas— when I was five years old—I was taken by my Uncle John to a side room to await Santa Claus' arrival, when I at once suggested that we should sing a song to surprise old Father Christmas as he passed the door. It was a German hunting song, which no doubt had its effect on our weird visitor, though my uncle could not give me a satisfactory answer on this head.

Although I was brimful of vitality when we left Germany, the climate began to tell upon me, as well as upon my mother ; and an attack of dysentery, which carried off hundreds of children, also left its effects upon my already nervous condition.   How trying the climate of the United States, with its dry electric quality and its extremes of heat and cold, is to some constitutions, is perhaps fairly well known.   I remember the weariness of those hot nights, and how one had to *rest* after getting up in the morning before one could dress ; and the winters were as severe in the opposite direction. On both my last visits to America, I felt the dryness and *excitingness* of the climate again, and could not stand it for longer than six months.   But I am not generally believed in England when I tell my friends that in Boston I lighted the gas by a touch of my finger on the metal of the gas jet, the spark elicited by the contact being sufficient to ignite it.

For the sake of my mother's and my health, then, my father deemed it his duty to leave America ; and he bethought himself of England.

My mother parted reluctantly from her pupils, but saw the necessity for a change ; and we again crossed the Atlantic, this time in a steamer, the *Herman*, leaving my uncle in America.   This was in May, 1857, my eighth birthday being spent on board ship.

We landed at Southampton ; and after looking round the town, which pleased him, my father determined to settle there. It must be a wealthy place, he thought, seeing how nicely dressed the people were. He found out his mistake soon enough.

Before settling down we spent ten days in London, sightseeing, during which time we lived in a small lodging-house in one of the courts leading out of Leicester Square.

Once settled in Southampton, my father was happier. The old country appealed to him, and made him feel nearer his own home; and he and my mother began to have confident hopes of the future. Some second-hand furniture was bought for the little house in Windsor Terrace, but my father hastened to make some that should be better. The first thing to be made, though, was a painted wire blind reaching half-way up the window, which bore the words, "Madame Josephine Herkomer, teacher of music;" and on either side of the inscription two figures growing out of ornament and blowing trumpets. The *artistic* touch could not be left out. Some chairs, a pretty table, and a sofa soon helped to furnish the drawing-room. Then my father set about getting work, and applied to one of the best decorating firms in the town, but without success. He was determined not to go to a shop to work like an ordinary workman, feeling that his duty lay at home in educating me and helping my mother in every way; and besides, his spirit revolted against it. Before long my mother had one pupil, and then a second through the recommendation of the first; and when Christmas came a few pupils were bringing in a small income. Such a small one! For my dear mother thought it

best not to charge too much, fifteen shillings a quarter
for two lessons a week, of an hour each !

The little money brought from America was spent,
but some neighbours, who took the trouble to know us,
insisted on lending us £5, that we might spend a happy
Christmas. Their name was Griffiths, and lodging with
them was a German merchant, Mr. Keller, who, unless
I am much mistaken, is at present German consul at
Southampton. He too had some hand in this loan.
Certainly these good people never did a kind act that
was better timed or more appreciated ; and as I write
these lines, I look back with the utmost emotion to that
Christmas—the first in a strange land—made happy by
these kind friends.

We bought the Christmas number of the *Illustrated
London News*, and I well remember the joy it gave
us. I was considered too old for a Christmas tree, but
at my urgent entreaty some thin pine boards were
bought me, out of which I could cut trees and animals.
My mother prepared some extra German dishes of some
farinaceous food, and I think on the whole it was a
happy Christmas ; though I remember her smiling
through tears.

But at my father's bench I was receiving the best
possible lessons, both for my hands and for my heart.
While my mother was giving her lessons, my father was
at his bench, making some furniture that should enable
him to show what he could do ; and a certain amount
of time he gave to the cooking, so as not to take my
mother away from her teaching, and at this duty I
assisted. But my mother often wanted my help, too,

finding me useful in singing with her pupils or in playing in the six-hand pianoforte pieces that were then so
fashionable. The musical taste of the period among
the middle classes was truly dreadful. "The Maiden's
Prayer"—does any one now remember that nauseous
and inane piece? I trust not. My mother tried to introduce better music among her pupils ; but the parents
complained, and the popular airs triumphed.

I regret to say that, much as I loved my mother, I
hated this sort of work, and felt a profound contempt
for the stupidity of the pupils, who were unable, after
repeated trials, to do what seemed to need no learning.

My father finished his cabinet, but not without alter-
ing the original design ; for the wood ran out, and
there was no money to buy more. So the ornament
round the top had to be made of the odds and ends
that were left. It was offered for sale for five pounds,
and exhibited in the windows of the decorating firm of
which I spoke before. But nobody bought it, or even
made an offer for it. I have it myself at the present
time, and could easily, to-morrow, get twenty times the
sum originally asked for it.

So my father had to work at such odd jobs as came
to him,—Oxford frames, with black nails at the corners,
for which he received seven shillings and sixpence each
for imperial size, and other such paltry work. Even
worse, work was offered him out of pity by well meaning friends of the pupils, such as framing and glazing
engravings in the common style. For one such commission, I remember, he had to carry a rather large
sheet of glass through the streets in a high wind. On

the way it broke, which meant a loss of two shillings. He went back to the shop and bought another piece, and this he brought safely home. I watched him, as he knelt down and laid it in the frame on the floor. Then he proceeded to put little nails all round the ends of the frame, as he thought necessary for keeping the glass down. It was a mistake ; for suddenly the glass cracked right across the centre. I see the poor man now, as he bent back with a loud cry of " Herr Gott !" Four shillings lost!—and he could only have obtained six for all, material and work together. Nor can I forget the suffering on his face when my mother came upstairs to see what was the matter.

It was suffering indeed. And there was no prospect of better things. My father still considered it his highest duty to look after my education, and stoutly resisted all advice or interference with his plans. As he was to strangers a silent, thoughtful man, they considered him rather proud. But he kept his own counsel, and saw further than others.

There was a break in the clouds for a short time when work came from a picture-cleaner, which sometimes brought in four pounds a week. The craze for old pictures was then at its height, and this pay still left a handsome profit to the man who gave him the work. But this did not last long, and the old state of things soon began again.

I received my first English lessons from a lady pupil of my mother's, in return for her music lessons. So much for work : while for entertainment there was always some pleasure and excitement to be got from the concerts which my mother gave with her pupils. I used to appear freely at them, singing songs, in character and with dramatic action, and playing the piano. My performances on this instrument were usually in six-hand pieces, in which I took the middle part, the treble and bass being given to girls. Crinolines were in all their glory, and each young lady did her best to smother me, so that nothing of me was visible but a black head of hair above a pile of muslin. One great service these juvenile appearances in public did me, in delivering me for all time from the nervousness from which many performers and speakers suffer. I have never been nervous before an audience in my life, and do not even know the feeling.

Music was always a part of my life; though I was never taught, and cannot remember how I learned my notes. I did not practise, but could generally do at once what my mother required of me, even while my thoughts were on my other work at my father's bench.

At my father's bench,—what a precious time it was for me! The influence of his companionship there belongs to the memories for which I have most reason to be thankful; and I see more and more daily how firmly his lessons took hold, and that they have borne good fruit. I had unbounded faith in him and admiration for him; nobody, I thought, that I had ever known or was ever likely to know, was so clever. The ideas that he expressed I quickly took up, and spread them enthusiastically among my playmates. Two lessons, though, I never could learn, hard as he tried to make me understand them : not to tell all one's thoughts, and not to give everything one had to other people. If I carved any little figure of an animal—as it usually was, —I had some one in my mind that I wanted to give it to before I had fairly coloured and set it on its stand. And if I got some fresh piece of information, I was longing to pass it on to some one who did not know it,— not in the way of telling secrets that I was told to keep, but from eagerness to impart my newly gained knowledge. It was from my mother decidedly that I inherited this: the trait was as strongly marked in her own character.

I was now about twelve years old, excessively restless and excitable, with already an extraordinary capacity for work, though but little power of sticking to one thing at a time—application, I suppose I should call it. No matter how the work of the day had been interrupted, some work *had* to be done, I felt, before going to bed. And a variety of work I did. I had quite a reputation among my playmates for making kites, and used to mend theirs for them, as well as making bows and arrows and crossbows, these last always with some carving on them. I used to carve figures of animals in the round, about six inches high, copying them from a book that some pupil of my mother's had given me; and always painted and textured them. Besides these, I did endless water-colour drawings, copied from the German " Bilderbogen," or from engravings in the *Illustrated London News*, consulting my father always upon the colours to be introduced into the various parts.

About this time my mother had a good many pupils, but they brought in but little, and the weekly income averaged about thirty shillings. There was no prospect of improvement for my father : now and then some better commission would come in, but it left him heart-sick, and he felt his best years passing without a chance of doing the good artistic work of which he knew himself capable. The general taste in matters of decorative art was thoroughly bad at the time. The Exhibition of 1851 only started a better feeling, and that of '62 gave it but a certain amount of additional impetus. The present favoured generation does not know how much it has to be thankful for. Carvers nowadays complain —I have heard them myself—that they cannot do their best work because they are cut down to the lowest penny in the payment by the contractors. But if this is so now, what was it like then, and above all in a country town like Southampton ?

An accident, trifling enough as it may sound, that happened about this time brought matters to a crisis. I was always sent to do the shopping, and on one of my errands I lost the half-sovereign that had been given me to change—the last gold that was in the house, or likely to be for some time. The disaster made it evident that something must be done to make my mother's hard-won earnings go farther. We were already as economical as possible ; but my father felt that a reduction *must* be made somewhere in the expenditure, and like a brave man he sacrificed himself, and gave up smoking, drinking, and meat-eating, and thus effected a saving of many shillings a week. That his health would not suffer from this change he argued from the fact that in his youth meat and beer were only indulged in on Sundays, and smoking was by no means universal.   But it was an act really heroic, and one that needed the strongest man to carry it through.   Total abstinence alone would have been hard enough ; its advocates in those days were thought fair game for scoffing and derision.   But smoking he found the hardest to give up.   When he had finished his last ounce of tobacco, he would walk behind some one who was smoking in the street to enjoy the smell, and it was many months before he found the smell of tobacco objectionable.   In place of meat he cooked himself farinaceous food, quite as nourishing, but less exciting to the system.   He allowed no one but himself to make the change of diet, insisting on my mother keeping to her usual food, with the glass of beer at dinner that her friends thought so necessary.   And hence arose some unhappy discussions.   My poor mother was anxious about my father's health, and could not help being influenced by her friends, who did all they could to frighten her and to persuade her that he was doing something not only unpardonably eccentric, but positively wicked.   For the belief in alcohol was only just beginning to be shaken, and that by a few enthusiasts, who had no medical evidence or sanction to support them, but who took a religious view of the matter.

My father bore it all patiently, argued gently but firmly with my mother, and said he would only try the experiment for a year : if he found it was doing him harm, he would return to his old diet.   As it happened, his appearance was affected by the sudden change quite as much as his feelings, though not in the same way. After a month he was distinctly better physically, but outwardly he was paler and thinner; which mattered very little to him, but was a bad sign-board for his new creed. A certain unhappiness came over my mother, she could not tell why; but my father gained a great sense of peace and contentment. I remember the change well. He became much more gentle and tender, was always in the same equable mood, very rarely put out or irritable. He seemed to gain a great mastery over himself. Here was matter for rejoicing enough, surely. But it was not until his colour returned that he could bring his wife or his few friends to see it in that light.

In renouncing tobacco and alcohol, my father left us a legacy of priceless value, and I hope that many generations may bless him for it, as I do now. He never urged the abstinence on me, but I was enthusiastic and devoted to him, and eagerly pressed it on others.

Even in our humble way things became brighter for us now, with the return of colour to my father's face. The money earned went further, and they were able to send me to a day-school.

I was at this school only a few months. I took it up eagerly and worked with feverish assiduity, and my easily over-wrought system collapsed. My excitability always prevented me from eating properly, and in spite of my father's constant attempts to make me sit out a meal, I was always on needles the whole time and impatient to rush off. This naturally affected my digestion, and the lowering of my system that resulted showed itself in a chronic abscess of some kind on my neck. It was nine months before this could be lanced, and even then it seemed to have been done too soon, as a

fresh one formed at once. The sense of disfigurement
made me shun people, and I was in a very low and
wretched state, from which I was rescued by a suggestion of my father's. He advised me to go out every
day, taking some food with me, and sit alone among
the trees on the neighbouring common, and there to
spend my time in thinking. This new track on which
he started me I hold to have been of the greatest use
to me in developing my mind. On the common, which
was a really fine piece of half-wild wood and open
country, a few miles from Southampton, I sketched a
little, but spent most of my time in watching nature
and giving myself up to the play of my imagination,
making worlds of my own and peopling them, and
coming home ever so happy at evening. I used to tell
my father my fancies, and he would always listen
gravely and attentively, and show me how they could be
applied to real life. My mother was rejoiced when she
heard me tell of the music that kept running through
my head ; for she secretly hoped that I should take to
music. Art had very little place in her mind, and
though she was proud of any work I did, and showed it
to every one, she was hoping in her heart of hearts that
music would be my vocation. This course of roaming
and ruminating in the open air rapidly improved my
health and developed my mind. I was now, in my
fourteenth year, sent to a school of art, one in connection with South Kensington, which I attended three
times a week. It was a great excitement, though not
unmixed with disappointment, for I was set to copy
those stupid outlines of casts ; and the master was a

man whose sole remark by way of criticism seemed to be : " Yes, that's all looking very nice." He was one of the first batch of masters sent out by the Science and Art Department, and was indeed a poor creature. Poor fellow ! He was an inveterate sketcher in water colours, and had a trick of touch (on the Harding model) for any tree he painted. At his death his sketches were put together and sold for so much per dozen. Such schools, with precisely the same examples and casts to copy, can be found in any town in England at this moment. As a rule the masters are better,— some indeed are good artists. But the gigantic machinery of South Kensington moves on in the same groove year by year ; the specimens of art for which prizes are given look every year the same, as if done by the same students. Nobody can change the system, nobody is responsible, and consequently nobody is to blame,—a most subtle contrivance.

In the evenings young mechanics or school teachers would come to the school to do chalk drawings from casts, and I was always amazed to see the points they made on their chalks—masterpieces in themselves. And then it was stipple, stipple, stipple, night after night, for six or perhaps nine months, at one piece of ornament something under fourteen inches long. The result would be duly sent in to headquarters and awarded a medal or what not, and the happy student would fancy himself an artist, and believe he had achieved something that meant the beginning of a great future in art. Alas ! how little did they know, or *can* they know now, of art, after such a deadening and petrifying operation. They cannot draw the simplest thing from nature. What have they learnt then? Nothing but a totally false conception of art, if any conception at all.

I went through the flat copies pretty fast; and then came stippling from casts; copies of those stupid life studies in coloured crayons by Mulready, and, above all, the water-colour drawings of my master, which I was allowed to take home to copy. Connected with this part of my studies was a little incident that occurs to me. There was a rather difficult water-colour given me to copy, which I could not manage at once. I started it two or three times, each time getting more excited and impatient; and at last, in a towering rage, I threw it up, and burst into tears, appealing to my father to try his hand at it. My poor mother stood by watching with sympathy, and weeping to keep me company, I fear—and so sorry for me! It happened that the quiet, steady, thoughtful way in which my father set about the copy irritated me, and I declared it was easy enough to do it "slowly like that." He went on without noticing my remark, and got it remarkably like the original, but not by the same method of touch. I started again, and got it right—aye, and straight off.

At the school I did the mask-head of Michael Angelo's Moses, and received a bronze medal for it. It was awarded me by Solomon Hart, R.A., who examined drawings at the schools throughout the country. The medal, I believe, was not willingly given by him for the drawing, but the master told him I was likely to go to Germany to study art, and he wanted me to have some honours to take with me from this school.

Now came the burning question of my future studies —in art: it was not to be music. The middle class and tradespeople that my mother had chiefly to deal with, knew so little about art that they thought it was hardly a respectable calling, and meant *certain* starvation. She, dear soul, thought they *might* be right, because she could not judge art at all herself, and was anxious for my future. There was in this way the outer influence working all the time against my father's clear and far-reaching sight. Some friends pressed my parents to let me enter the Ordnance Survey Office in the town, where I would be sure to rise soon, and where my future would be secured, as pensions always followed after thirty or forty years' service. Thirty or forty years! It would be a comfort to think of, and would relieve my parents, once for all, of anxieties for my future. Thus argued our friends! But my father's answer was short, and almost fierce: "No," he said; "my son shall be a free artist, and not a slave!" They shrugged their shoulders, shook their wise heads, and made my poor mother weep. Brave woman that she was, she could not be expected to see a future which she did not understand. It was doubly hard for her to bear as almost our entire income came from her teaching. The future seemed so uncertain, and there seemed no way out of the depressing state of our life. What made matters worse for my father, was, that my mother's sister and husband (Mr. and Mrs. Wurm), came over from Germany to settle in England. They were musicians, and being at that time *very* "green" and inexperienced, they put all their weight against my father's

M

decision for my future.   Mr. Wurm, whom I greatly
respect now, may hardly remember saying to my father
that I would never succeed as an artist, and that my
father, in his judgment, was taking away my chances of
success in music, for which he thought me better fitted.

We had in the meantime moved to a better street, and
occupied one house with my uncle and aunt—who by
that time were doing fairly well as teachers of German
and music.   In this house I annoyed my uncle very
much by my solos on the penny whistle, on which I
prided myself as being a virtuoso !

It was in the spring of 1865 that things came to a
climax.   The key that turned events came in the shape
of a commission from Uncle John in America, for the
four Evangelists to be carved in wood—life size, after the
models of Peter Vischer in Nürnberg.   This opened out
a chance for my father to take me to Munich to study
art, as he could work at this commission, for which my
uncle was able to advance money.

My mother desired to remain with her pupils, to earn
the money that was so precious.   We started early in
the spring for Germany, being armed with passports (as
English naturalized subjects), and with little money,
but with hope in our hearts.   Parting from my mother
was hard, but it was considered that art must be my
vocation, and every sacrifice must be made for my
education.

We crossed to Antwerp on a steamer that had a cargo
of sheep, and the rough sea, combined with the stench
from the closely packed sheep, made me dreadfully sick.
We stayed but a few hours in Antwerp, and then made

our way into Germany through Elsass and Lothringen. I cannot think now what tour that could have been. All I can remember is the vulgarity and bestial habits of the people that travelled with us in the third and fourth class. All these cheap trains were of the slowest kind. But somehow or other we got into Switzerland, for I remember bathing in the lake of Luzern, and then nearly fainting—for a heavy illness was upon me. We then passed to Kempten, to visit my Uncle Wurm's old mother, who lived in a neighbouring village. I was undoubtedly ill, for something in the old lady's face shocked and frightened me, and in spite of all her offers of hospitality, I urged my father to stay the night in Kempten. This was a two hours' walk. In this walk, as I held on to my father's arm, I seemed to fall into a curious sleep—notwithstanding the action of walking; my father's voice every now and again seemed quite distant, and sometimes I did not hear him at all. We arrived late at a hotel in Kempten, and as the cheap rooms were under repairs, we were put into a large and more expensive bedroom. I slept right through the night without waking once ; but in the morning, when my father awakened me, I found I could not raise my head. The illness was upon me ; what it was I do not know, but it was a terrible sensation of sickness, an agony which turned my face to a purple colour. The despair of my poor father was intense. His troubled mind saw the slender means at our disposal drift away, for the illness threatened a prolonged stay in the place. He applied what he knew to be efficacious before in cases of illness in the family, viz., the wet sheet, or hydropathic cure, a system that was started in Germany, just before we left, by an inspired peasant called Priessnitz. The keeper of the hotel supplied us with the blankets and sheets, and I was " packed up."

Before me on the wall was a picture of a woman—child in her arms, lost in the snow, ringing at a bell (attached to a cross) for help. This was dismal to look at ; but harder to bear was the sight of my poor distressed father, who nursed me with the tenderness of a woman. Towards the evening I was so much better that my father could take me, or rather carry me, to the fresh air. Another night of " packs," with intervals of sleep for me but none for my watchful father, enabled us to move forward. I rapidly mended ; and on settling in Munich with the prospects of studying art seriously, my joy was great.

As economy was our first thought, it was deemed necessary to have all we needed in one room. In a back building ("Rückgebaüde") belonging to a master carpenter, whose workshop was below us, we rented a room which was to serve as bedroom, carving room, kitchen and sitting-room. It had one of those German (modern) iron stoves in it, which could be used for heating and cooking.

The rough part of the carving work my father arranged to do in the workshop below, and the finer carving only in our own room. Such a craving as I had for work and study was surely never surpassed by any young man not yet sixteen years old. I hungered for work. It must be told that on our arrival I joined the preparatory school for the academy schools, but it was

Portrait of my father from my oil painting done in 1881.

only for a week previous to its closing for holidays. During that week I did a chalk drawing of the head of Demosthenes, from the cast, and received the highest approval of my master, Professor Echter. This lovable man, a pupil of Kaulbach (and the one who executed all those Kaulbach Frescoes at Berlin), took a great fancy to me.

During the long vacation he allowed me to go to his studio and take home casts to draw from. This was all very well, but I longed to draw from the human figure, and it was my good father who first sat to me for such study. We rose at six o'clock every morning ; we then washed in cold water all over ; and whilst I dressed, my father made the fire in the stove, and put the water on to boil. During that time my father remained un-dressed, and in the intervals of his domestic work posed for me. When the water boiled, it was time to lay aside the sketch, but to be renewed the next morning. Surely this is as touching as anything can be ! As he dressed I made the bed, and then we both got the breakfast and sat down to eat, with alternate looks at the sketch. After breakfast father would go on with his figures, and I with my casts, to please Professor Echter. My whole character had changed with this new life. That restlessness and over excitability seemed to subside, and there never was a thought of crossing the wishes of my parents, which I fear was not the case in my earlier years, though there never was anything wilful in my boyish disobedience. I was considered an exemplary son and worker. But the art students I had seen in that week at school had no faith in me, because

I did not wear long hair, a big brimmed hat (like Buffalo Bill's), and a shawl thrown over my shoulders. Every student in those days had these accessories. Nor was industry a point of honour with them, but quite the reverse ; hence the surprise and disbelief in me. I was not eccentric, and was unpardonably industrious.

As this kind of study from the cast became irksome to me, my father joined, with me, and for my sake, a private evening class for drawing from the nude figure, both male and female. Here artists came to keep up their practice, and a pretty queer lot of drawings they made. But the delight was great to me.

In the daytime I paid regular visits to the various picture galleries of old and new masters.

I had now a craving to do something *original.* But how to go to work I did not know. I could not ask Professor Echter, because he already disliked my drawing from the life. At that time the cry was, " Nature is all very well, but Kaulbach is better." He used Nature up to a certain point only, and then completed it by copying casts from the antique.

How to produce something original ! A burning thought. Little did I think *Nature* herself produces the materials for the expression of originality : nobody told me this. My father tried to advise, but was only too anxious to be informed on the subject himself. I tried putting together things out of various prints. But it was not satisfactory, and I was by no means sure that the result was original after all.

In spite of small means we had much happiness. We heard military music a good deal, and went to the standing-place (the cheapest) of the "Hof-Theater." It was the first time I had heard an opera or had seen a play. 'Preciosa'—a drama, with incidental music by Weber, was the first musical play I saw. It had a magical effect upon me, and threatened hard to take my thoughts from my art work. We also saw 'Der Freischütz,' when the present famous singer, Vogl, made his first appearance on the stage. I had no piano, therefore piano playing was entirely forgotten, nor was there any desire to take up that branch of music. I did, however, wish I could compose music.

We wrote home once a week to mother, and I rejoice to say that I wrote good letters to her, full of love and devotion. I found one of these letters not long ago, in which I asked her to forgive me for all the trouble I had given her in my former thoughtless years, and said that I would in future always think of how I could make her and my father happy.

We had also seen my father's brother, the doctor, which gave my father much pleasure. I was much interested in his anatomical talks.

The Evangelists were about half done when we found our passports had to be renewed, as they were only issued, in those days, to naturalized subjects for six months at a time. To our dismay we found they had to be renewed in person in England. So it meant that we and the unfinished Evangelists had to return to England or else forfeit our English citizenship, with the other alternative of exposing me to military duties. It was a blow, but there was no help for it. The clumsy Evangelists were packed in rough boxes, and we re-

turned without delay. Of the return journey I remember absolutely nothing, but I do remember my
father's words as we met my mother again : " There,
dear wife, I bring you a tall boy."

In Southampton a schoolroom, which of course I
shared, was rented for the carving work. Through this
winter I did all sorts of work. I sketched, in pencil, all
our friends who were willing to sit. They were *always*
good likenesses, but were not artistic. I did a good
deal of casting of leaves from nature by a process I
learnt in Munich, and gave a set of them to the School
of Art in Southampton.

It was now decided that I should be sent to the South
Kensington schools. Through the recommendation of
one of mother's pupils, we heard of a good house for me
in Wandsworth Road. It was the house of a retired
carpenter. He and his wife were indeed good to me.
They made me one of the family, and only charged a
very small fee. But it was a three-mile walk to the
Kensington schools, and this journey I did four times a
day. My father came up with me from Southampton,
and Mr. Hall showed us the nearest way, on a bitterly
cold March day, to Kensington. After having settled
the fee at the schools, I walked back with my father as
far as the statue of Achilles in Hyde Park. There, in
front of that statue, I parted with my father for the first
time in my life, and returned to the schools with the
new sensation of being left alone amongst strangers in a
big city.

At the schools I showed my life studies from Munich
to one of the teachers, who pooh-poohed them in

right English fashion. He did not believe in these foreign schools; but what he did believe in were the outlines from the antique, which were distributed throughout the English Science and Art schools. He was the draughtsman of those outlines. I might go into the antique room I was told, but the life class was out of the question. Had the master shown any kindness to me, I might have taken his directions more willingly. As it was I was galled. In the antique I therefore started a figure, but during the hours of rest I wandered into the life class, where Luke Fildes, R.A., Henry Woods, A.R.A., John Parker, R.W.S., and others were working. This was too much for me to see and to be debarred from. I brought my easel over, and straightway began a life drawing in chalk. As luck would have it, I had half done my figure before a master came. A Mr. Herman came first, and fumed. The master Collinson followed, and uttered some surprise at my audacity. Then finally came the head master, Burchett, and looked carefully at the drawing, and then at me. He said I had infringed a rule, but as the drawing was good, I might stay in the life class! Here was a triumph over the others in the antique class, who would have liked to have done the same thing, but hadn't the pluck or the audacity. I always respected the rules of an institution, but I felt an injustice had been done me by one of the masters, to which I would not submit willingly.

I worked very industriously here, and improved rapidly. Some of the life studies were very good, others were weak in colour though good in drawing. But *none* were vigorous and strong. I adopted an insipid grey paper, in imitation of some of the students, and messed up black and white chalk upon it. Some of the best work was done at night, in colour, by gaslight. This went on for the term of five months in the summer of 1866.

Then I returned to Southampton, formed a life class on the suggestion of a student who was formerly in the School of Art with me, and showed my fellow-workers all I knew or had learnt at Kensington. Our combined works were exhibited at a frame-maker's shop. This show was tolerably good. Landscapes predominated, especially by one of the members, who painted under the influence of Ruskin's writings. At this distance I cannot judge them, but as far as I can remember, all colours seemed to have been used in their full strength. Purple was the main colour of the shadows.

I was influenced by this, although I had never read Ruskin, but I took the gospel from this fellow-student, who was an ardent admirer of his. It was a great mistake, and it took years to wean me from the purple in my shadows. At this exhibition I sold my first picture, a little water-colour landscape, for £2 2s.

Of all the exhibitors I was the only one who gave up my whole time to art. The others were map-engravers (the Ruskin advocate), builders, gilders, and so on—about seven or eight of us.

At this period I also gave drawing lessons and music lessons, and did what I could to earn some money. In the summer of 1867 I had another term at Kensington. It was then I received the influence that has biassed all my art work—no influence of that stupid school, Heaven knows! but the influence of the works of Frederick Walker. His 'Bathers' had already been exhibited in the Old Academy in Trafalgar Square, and although hung over a doorway, at once heralded a new departure in English art. There were hot discussions in the life-room at Kensington about Walker's work. It was flat, chalky, and ill-drawn to some ; to others it had the light of Nature, and was above all things unconventional. I can remember nothing of the pictures in that exhibition except Walker's 'Bathers,' and Poynter's 'Israelites in Egypt.' Nor can I remember that Millais was much talked about amongst students at Kensington. All I know is that we devoured Walker's wood-engraving, and looked upon him as the man to follow. I soon tried my hand at a wood-drawing, and the subject was a little girl watching a pie placed on a table under a tree in a garden, with a hidden stick under her apron, ready for the cat (up the tree), should it attempt to touch the pie which was to cool in the air. Not a poetic subject, but it was the first. Fildes at that time was our authority on wood-drawing, as he had done much in illustrations, and copied a good many pictures on the block for the *Illustrated London News.* One morning in the galleries, as he was copying Armitage's 'Judas with the Priests,' I showed him the block. He said little about it either one way or the other, but was on the whole rather inclined to favour it. I tried to get it taken by the editor of some children's magazine, but failed.

After July I returned to Southampton. Now came a

curious windfall through a literary friend, named Eustace Hinton Jones, who wrote for London papers. He recommended me as cartoon draughtsman for a new comic paper started by the late Hain Friswell. Two pounds a week for the one drawing, as a certainty, seemed a fortune. I did a cartoon of 'Death and Folly feeding War,' of Bradlaugh besmearing a figure of Truth, and several others, connected with the fall of Queen Isabella of Spain.

After about six weeks the paper collapsed. On the recommendation of the same friend, I did some drawings for the comic paper *Fun*.

In the summer of '68, I started my first sketching adventure, across the water, in a place called Hythe. Some way inland stood a windmill, with two deserted and dilapidated cottages adjoining it. I selected in these cottages, by the miller's permission, the only room that still retained its door and nearly all the panes of glass to the window, for my bedroom. I arranged to take my meals in one of the cottages nestling in the trees some hundred yards off.

The hostess was a grim, bony, masculine woman, who whipped her husband, and brought her drunken son, of twenty-three, home with a stick. To me she was uniformly kind, and would have flogged any man who touched " her young gentleman," as she called me. My food was simple : for dinner I had potatoes (boiled in their jackets) and milk ; for breakfast and supper, milk and bread and butter, and sometimes tea or little things sent me from home.

I started a sunrise landscape in water colour, and rose

from my bed of straw at 2.30 each morning. The picture represented a valley stretching out to sea, with the mists of early morning hanging round. The evenings were spent in the old woman's cottage ; the miller played the fiddle, and I played the zither, which latter certainly took the palm. The old miller was quite a character. He never undressed to sleep, washed his face and hands at the brook, and used sand for soap, which he greatly recommended. It was before the days of Pears' soap. But strange to say, I never attempted to sketch him, or any other of the characteristic people about me. Only landscape took my fancy, and children. I painted this landscape, and introduced into it two children. I also painted a poor cabbage garden, with a girl about to choose one to cut. Both these were sent to the Dudley Gallery and hung, but not well. Of the latter picture, a paper said, " It represents an ugly girl, choosing bad cabbages, with an impossible background." This picture I sold for two or three pounds to my friend, Mr. E. H. Jones, who sent it a few years later to Christie's, where it fetched £25.

During this visit I drew two or three blocks, and one represented a little girl with a pitcher, pushing aside the boughs as she was coming away from the brook. It was a good drawing, and was afterwards published in *Good Words*, with a story written to it, called ' Lonely Jane.' I sent this and the other blocks to the Dalziel Brothers, hoping they would buy them. I received an immediate reply, enclosing the money, and hoping I would supply them with more work. This was my first introduction to these two men, who so befriended me in after years, and to whom I shall always feel a great debt of gratitude.

During the winter I produced little. I gave music lessons and drawing lessons, painted portraits, and tried to do wood drawings, but things did not look bright. I felt I must go to London, to be nearer the publishers for wood-drawing. I carried my point to move up to London and try my luck, but my parents were much against it.

I took lodgings with a fellow-student who lived at Clapham, and was to work with me at 32, Smith Street, Chelsea. He was a jovial fellow, who took life heartily, and we laughed and were merry in our empty room. There was a box and a chair in it, and I sat on the chair, and placed my zither on the box, and played in the empty room to our intense satisfaction. I think my fellow-student sat on the floor. We had one bit of carpet, about a yard long, which amused us some time, as we endeavoured to find out where it would " tell " best.

Soon the parents sent me a few things of furniture— a folding bed, and some saucepans, etc., because I thought *I* could do the cooking. It was a beastly *ménage* that we had, and the horrors of washing up always caused trouble, because my comrade would not willingly do his share of house-work. I would have to give him the towel in his hand, or a saucepan to scrape ; and be it told to our everlasting disgrace, that we made parcels of our saucepan scrapings and dropped them down the areas of respectable houses on dark nights.

We must now needs do a picture together, and have

a model. He was all for the classic, so we invented a subject of a Greek girl dropping bread into a pool of water, feeding the fish. I started a water colour, and he an oil picture. Mine was eccentric, and his commonplace. The model was a Frenchwoman, and was such a "swell," that neither of us had the courage to offer her the money for the sittings. I bethought me of a dodge, and asked for her purse; but this only aroused her suspicions—why should *I* want her purse? She *was* paid, however, and with it we abandoned the Greek girl, subject and model.

I did what I could in drawing subjects to have stories written to them, and Dalziel's did all they could for me, but failed to get rid of many of the blocks. I did one very fair drawing, of a pretty girl dreaming among some ruins, and tried my luck with Cassell's. After some delay I was ushered into the presence of Mr. Petter, then one of the active partners. With him sat a servile editor, whose business it seemed to be to echo Mr. Petter's words. I showed my block; they put their heads together; Petter mumbled something, which was acquiesced in by violent assenting nods of the editor's head.

Petter.—"H'm. Is this your first drawing, young man?"

H.—"No, sir; I have done many for Messrs. Dalziel Brothers."

They look at each other and shake their heads.

P.—"We can do *nothing* with this drawing. The fact is you want to eat a little more pudding!" To the editor: "Eh! a little more pudding?"

Editor.—" Yes ; I should say a *good deal* more pudding."

They nod together and laugh.

H.—" Thank you ; give me my block."

P.—" You see, we give you good advice, and I should further advise you to study anatomy. Anatomy is sadly lacking in . . ."

H.—" Good-day."

And I bolted, with the word " brute " choking me. I have given this in full, for it burned itself into my memory. If editors and managers would only remember that they may be dealing with men who are destined to succeed, and who remember kindness as keenly as they do cruelty, they would be more courteous to strange " young men," or at least more cautious.

What I was now to do for money I did not know. My companion stayed for no meals, except for a cup of tea now and again! and I limited myself to porridge and tea. I could not ask the parents to help me further, and I made pretence that things were all right. I took my zither to some christy minstrels that were performing in St. George's Hall, and asked for engagement. At that moment they had no vacancy, but they wished me to call again the following week. In the meantime I heard of some stencilling work to be done at South Kensington at ninepence an hour. I obtained this, and worked at it with a fellow-student. We worked any number of hours, but produced little. Then they made it " piecework," under which arrangement we produced too much in the time. But I could not stand the slavery of this mean work, which is at the present moment to be seen around the Ceramic Gallery at the South Kensington Museum. My companion thought it best to keep on, but I felt it derogatory to my condition (poor as it was), and struck.

The *Graphic* newspaper having been started, I thought it best to try and get employment there. Precious little money had I in hand, but I was able to pay £1 for a full-page block, and had just enough to pay for the models to carry out my subject. I chose for subject, 'Gipsies on Wimbledon Common.' This block I took, with much trepidation of heart, to the *Graphic* office. At the top of the stairs on the second floor is a room with one engraver in it. He took the block to the manager, Mr. W. L. Thomas, and soon returned with the message that the manager wanted to see me.

Mr. Thomas, who was leaning over my drawing as I entered, half turned on his stool and shook hands with me. He seemed surprised that he had not heard of me, because the drawing was so good, he said. He accepted the block there and then, and said he would be pleased to take any amount of such good work from me. How I thrilled with excitement and joy, and the two flights of stairs in going down seemed so different—or my legs did ; two and three steps at a time, out into the street, home to Chelsea—to write the great news to my parents! Eight pounds I received for that block ! From this time I never lacked work.

E. F. Brewtnall, myself, and another student, by name Wise, accepted an invitation to spend the autumn of this year for sketching at the home of a fellow-student, whose parents promised to put us up cheaply. This was

N

a happy time for all.   I started a full imperial size water-colour drawing of some figures in a field, hoeing, with a distance of trees in autumn colours.   Brewtnall also started a large water-colour—the return of labourers to their cottages.   Wise did smaller things, and looked to the painting more than to subject.   Here my zither again enlivened the evenings.

Brewtnall wrote some verses, which I put to music, and the chorus ran thus :

> " One was a yeoman, stalwart and bold,
>   One was a German, a regular beau,
>   One was a Saxon, with hair like gold,
>   And the other was a knight from Pimlico."

This represented the company, Rassall, our host, myself, Brewtnall, and Wise.   The verses related the terrible result of all four men falling in love with the one girl in the house, who was an orphan child brought up by the Rassalls.   Wise *did* afterwards marry her.

After this pleasant campaign, the others went back to London, but I first paid a visit to my parents in Southampton, to show them what I had done.

My coming home was an event.   It was late after-noon when I arrived, but I quickly unpacked the picture and hung it on the wall, whilst there was still daylight left for the parents to see it.   They were surprised, and my father drew me into his arms for an embrace ; but he did not speak.   Later on he told me how happy he felt that I was now really able to paint " a picture." He had a surprise for me, too, an old-fashioned high-backed settle, which he made for me and had just

finished on the day of my visit. This was placed
behind the little table upon which was spread the
supper. The dear mother had sent away her pupils
that afternoon early, to enable her to cook me some
special dishes (German dishes) that she knew I liked
much. There was a spotless white cloth, some flowers,
and two candles. We *were* indeed happy—we three!

It was during this period that I made the first drawing of my 'Chelsea Pensioners in Church,' carefully
drawn, but badly enough engraved. However, enough
of it was left to make a decided mark in the *Graphic*
newspaper.

Now came the spring of 1870, and with it the time
for sending our pictures to the Dudley Gallery, which
was at that time the only available Exhibition for out-
siders. We had little hopes of having them hung, on
account of their size. Daily we expected the letter
of rejection. At last a letter came to me with the
Dudley Gallery mark on it. My heart sank. I opened
it, and found—*not* a notice of rejection, but a letter
from the Secretary asking me to call on him. I rushed
into Brewtnall's lodgings, showed him the letter, and
asked if he understood it? He did not; but he
thought it serious! So did I. Arriving at the Gallery,
I was ushered into the smallest of rooms, where sat the
Secretary. He got up and shook hands with me, and
said he was "glad to make my acquaintance," and
I felt inclined to say, "Not half so glad as I was to
make his." He then told me privately that my picture
was hung in the place of honour, and that he wished
me to raise the price. I had put £20 on it; he advised

£40. My good fortune I owed to H. S. Marks, R.A., and Arthur Severn, both strangers to me.   My friends the Dalziels now stepped forward and advised Strahan, the publisher, to buy it.   I was thus able to help my parents ; but my mother would not give up her teaching.   My father, however, started in good earnest to make furniture for me for which I determined to build a great house some day.

In the summer of 1870 I went to a fishing village on the coast of Normandy, not far from Dieppe.   I painted an elaborately designed scene in water colour of the fisher-folk on the beach, the principal group clustering around a young fisher-girl reading news of the coming war with Germany.   It was a good piece of grouping, but the workmanship was hard and thin. On the declaration of war, I thought it safest to beat a retreat, because all knew I was a German.   They pitied me, as a German, because they were going to give Germany a tremendous beating.   On all sides I heard only this version.   This water colour was bought by E. Dalziel for £50.   It was hung well in the Dudley in 1871.   On the strength of this and another drawing, I was invited, by the Institute of Painters in Water Colour, to join their ranks without competition.   E. J. Gregory, who had become well known from his excellent drawings in the *Graphic*, was similarly invited with me. Gregory and I were boys together in Southampton, and it is a satisfaction to me to think of my words to his mother when the question of his art career was put to me for decision.   I said, " He has more real talent than any of us."

Through the winter of 1870, and the opening of 1871, I did much wood drawing. I also painted a water-colour drawing of my 'Chelsea Pensioners in Church,' for Mr. W. L. Thomas of the *Graphic*. I had now put by enough money, as I thought, to take my father to Germany for six months. My mother rejoiced to think my father would have a real holiday.

The Bavarian highlands! Ah! that was a dream. I felt sure I could treat those peasants in the artistic spirit of Walker, and it was a new field for an English artist. We started in the spring, and travelled very differently to the first time I visited Germany. We reached Garmisch, near Partenkirchen, and I knew it was the right spot. We took lodgings in a peasant's house, occupying one of those large rooms with endless windows, and containing two bedsteads of abnormal shortness, each with a feather bed that reached from the chin to the knee, and stood up about eighteen inches in the middle. My father did our cooking during this visit.

We were quite happy together. I had now, for the first time in my life, felt the real charm of a German pine forest and of mountain scenery. I started a large water colour of a beautiful old well, with various figures grouped around it. Also a smaller subject in water colour. But I itched to try my hand at oil colour, and sent to Munich for materials. But, strange to say, I had forgotten my Kensington practice in oils. I was the water colour painter, therefore tried to get my oil paint-ing to look as much like water colour as possible. To accomplish this, I used benzine as a medium. My subject was old and young men sitting outside their houses after work. The figures were half life size, and were all portraits ; but it was an awkward composition. I also drew a couple of blocks for the *Graphic*, thus keeping up the finances. But one day I saw, to my dismay, that the money would not hold out. The money for the blocks could not be expected before they were accepted. So I wrote to my good friend Dalziel, and asked him to advance me £25, to be repaid directly I sold my pictures. He at once sent me the money "with pleasure," he said. The return was now safe. We had some lovely times there together— my father and I. He, with his romantic fancies, and I, the young ardent spirit, blended well together. We often made our meals out in the forest, and the principal charm of this was making a fire by the running brook of crystal water.

I played the zither a great deal during that stay, and became very dexterous on it. When the snow came we thought it time to push homeward again.

At home I soon sold my pictures, repaid Mr. Dalziel, and made my plans for the next year. But a curious incident happened to me that winter. Mr. Marks, one of the few friends of note I had at that time, came to see my work, and he advised me not to exhibit the oil picture, but to withdraw it altogether. I took his advice, and believe my future was immeasurably benefited by this action. He knew I would do something so much better the next year—and so I did. This first oil picture was cut up, and only the heads of the figures were kept.

Before the next spring (1872), partly through my pictures, and partly through much wood drawing, I had saved £200. Now I was able to give my mother a real holiday as well as my father, and it was arranged that we three should make a stay of six months again in the same place, Garmisch. I had collected all this money in gold to show my mother, and we placed it in little piles on the table as we counted it. I think I have never felt so rich since, certainly no money ever gave me so much happiness. This time I determined to do an oil picture of six feet long, as it was time to make my appearance in the Royal Academy.

I still intended to introduce the old men resting on a bench outside their houses, and designed the whole subject during the winter at home, as I knew exactly what I should find on the spot. 'After the Toil of the Day,' it was called, and represented a street with old, sunburnt, wooden houses on the one side, and a river bordered with apple-trees on the other. The old people and the children were sitting on the benches, with more able-bodied peasants returning from the fields. It was the spirit of Walker that entirely guided my feelings in this picture. Although thoroughly Bavarian, and although painted on the spot direct from Nature, I had in it two strong points that indicated Walker, viz., the apple-trees and a herd of geese. The effect was evening, thus enabling me to get Walker's warmth of colour. I painted it on an absorbent ground, made by my father, which gave it that *dry*, fresco-like appearance that I thought so essential, in those days, to oil painting. And although it was *flat*, and wanting

in what we now talk so much about—" planes " and
" values "—it certainly had a charm in its quality not
to be replaced by mere photographic realism. Faces
were carefully stippled up as in water colour, and there
was in the workmanship that odd admixture of ex-
cessive finish with undue sketchiness.

The six months in Garmisch were most successful ;
there was nothing to disturb us. I had means enough
at hand, and knew how to get money under an emer-
gency. My mother played duets on the piano, and I
composed duets for the zither, my second zither player
being an official's wife, who played well. This gave
the evenings a domestic as well as musical tone. My
father divided his time between sketching in water
colours and helping me by making whatever I needed
in matters of easels, grounds, etc.

With the snow we again came back to England, my
parents to Southampton, and I to my rooms in Chelsea,
which were uniquely furnished with my father's carved
furniture. I had also built a small glass-house studio
in the back garden—twenty-five feet long and eight
feet wide. The end was all glass, which gave me the
daylight effect on the models.

In the winter of this year I painted many water-
colour drawings,—some realistic subjects, some fanciful.
Amongst them was a Fairy Allegory, with a great deal
of hidden meaning in it, not quite clear to myself. This
picture found much favour when it was exhibited at
the Institute of Painters in Water Colours, and the flat
gold frame, with the butterflies painted on it, attracted
much attention. This butterfly fancy was not an imita-

tion of Whistler, for at that time I had not known of his existence. In the *very small* art circle, in which I moved, he was not spoken of then. Much had to be done during that winter to finish the large oil picture. Although I was anxious to sell it, I knew I could live on my wood-drawing and on the sale of small water colours. It was pure ambition that made me venture on a big picture. I knew *if* such a large picture *was* successful, I would make my mark quickly. Although the private purchaser was not much thought about, I could not help feeling a desire to send it into the Academy sold. I offered it first to a man who had bought many of my water colours; but he haggled about the price, and offered a sum which was £20 below what I wanted.

The curious accident that brought me a purchaser ought to be recorded. I was one day going to the Old Masters' Exhibition, and rode in the omnibus with my frame-maker. A gentleman in the 'bus, hearing our art talk, joined in the conversation. He said he lived in Sloane Square, and possessed many landscapes by Nasmyth. I again met the gentleman in the Academy Exhibition looking at the Old Masters. I thought it no harm to invite him to see my picture. The morning before he came he sent a note to ask if he might bring a friend? Certainly, only too glad. He brought Mr. Waller, the builder, whose workshops adjoined the end of my garden in Smith Street. They evidently liked the picture. Soon after Mr. Waller asked if *he* might bring a client of his, and he brought Mr. C. W. Mansel Lewis, who bought the picture for £500, and at the same time gave me a commission for another for £250.

Mr. Lewis has remained my staunch friend ever since. He is a man of infinite taste, and of much ability as an artist. He has been my companion in my camping expeditions, and has himself been an exhibitor in the Academy.

The picture 'After the Toil of the Day' was hung on the line in the Academy in 1873, and was well received, but it was so like Walker in feeling that I frequently heard the remark of passers-by, " Oh, here's a Walker! "

With the sum of £500 I was now able to open an account at a bank. This also brought me to the serious thought of settling down somewhere with my parents. My mother was loth to give up her teaching and her in- dependence; but it had been my most cherished wish to make a home for them, a home that I could share with them. My father was happy in his work, and I felt sure that the task of weaning my mother from her work was only a matter of time, for she was far from strong. I have inherited her ceaseless energy, and could well understand her dread of what she called an *idle life* in depending wholly on me. But I longed for her to feel some happiness *in depending* upon her son !

Her leave-taking from her pupils was touching, for they knew and appreciated her goodness and beauty of character. She then put together all her books, and counted up the total amount she had earned in teaching from the time we left Germany to the time she gave up teaching to please me. These books are the sweetest legacies she could have left me. Self-sacrifice for and unbounded kindness to others were her strong points. She had a pure mind, with a strange touch of the

rait of myself at one year old from a drawing
from life made by my father

spiritual, which gave her a sensitiveness not possessed by many. No matter how far she was away from me, she always knew to the hour when I fell ill. Always ailing a little, and often in much pain, she was never known away from her post at the piano for more than a day. My father's exceptionally tender nursing certainly helped much towards this.

I rented a cottage in Bushey, near Watford, for my parents, where I thought to live and work when I was not in town. It was the winter of 1873. And now, simultaneously with this came the event that was the sole source of all my greatest sorrow in life, and which threatened to break up my existence and destroy all that I cherished. I was very inexperienced then in matters of society ; I had a very limited circle of friends, and those not all of the right kind. Then it was I met the woman who was to take me through all my heaviest sufferings. But for the timely help of two rare friends, ten long years of trial would have killed me. I wish to relate as little as possible of this unhappy marriage to a woman, who was well-educated, but was an *invalid*, body and mind. The fancied wrongs of *her* life were the springs that let loose my pity, and from the highest motives of self-sacrifice, I thought I was doing a worthy thing in trying to make one person happy who had not known happiness, according to her version. I was wrong. Chaos followed everything she touched, and her mind was unable to see anything in its true light. Add to this the congestion of the lungs which left her prostrate soon after the marriage, and the beginning of my troubles can be imagined. I worked at her bedside,

so as to keep the expenses from over-weighting the income. As she was progressing towards recovery, a new
trained nurse came—a Miss Lulu Griffiths, who had
made nursing her life's work long before it was fashionable for ladies to become nurses, as we find, fortunately,
now-a-days. She had been lady probationer for a year
at Middlesex Hospital, and then took the ordinary
nursing to do there for practice. She was a splendid
surgical nurse, and this first appearance in our family
has to be noted, as she will often be mentioned later on
in these pages.

I took my wife to the Alps for a change—to Ramsau
in the Bavarian Alps. The *return* journey cost me £300,
as I had to satisfy all her most extravagant fancies. I
could not, nor would I, judge which were the fancies
and which the real necessities. This homeward journey
took five weeks.

I painted a couple of water-colours in Ramsau, but
soon found I could not leave my wife's side, because,
after every short absence, I found the lodging-house
keeper up in arms about something or other.

On the 8th of December a boy was born, in Bushey.

I had missed a year in the Academy, much to my
regret, but my domestic troubles quite prevented me
from attempting a big picture. I had set my heart on
painting the 'Chelsea Pensioners in Church' on a large
scale, in oils, on a canvas eight feet high.

Mr. W. L. Thomas of the *Graphic* was most emphatic
about this attempt being a mistake, saying the red coats
could not be managed on a large scale. Every other
friend I consulted warned me against attempting it. I

listened to all, but I set my teeth and vowed I *would* do it.

About the middle of December I had not done more towards it than stretch the canvas. If I missed another year at the Academy, my career would be thrown back ten years, I thought, and events have proved that I judged rightly. On the 1st of January I made the first real start on the picture, having arranged my little Chelsea garden studio, so as to get the same light on the figures as in the church. The two principal figures that sat for the drawing still lived, and I painted those in first. Never, probably, was so important a picture worked out in such a way. No design was made of the groups, and no measurements taken of the architectural perspective. On the white canvas I sketched the central (dying) figure, and the big man on the seat in front of him. I merely guessed at the probable correct sizes and distances between the figures. Then came the figure next to the central man, the one that looks into his face, alarmed, and touches his arm to see what the matter is. Then the figure next to the bald-headed man in the front seat. I always had two men together, to see how one face came against the other.

It must be told that there was *no* oil colour ground on the canvas ; it was a piece of unprepared linen, with nothing but a coating of size. Each figure was sketched on it with zinc white mixed with paste, using water-color lampblack and raw sienna for the outlines. This produced that dry, fresco-like appearance, but it was too absorbent, and necessitated the use of much medium to secure the paint on the canvas, as the ground *drew out* too much of the binding material in the colours. It was not until it had been soaked with medium five or six times, back and front, after it was finished, that the paint ceased to *chip* in places.

I could not work at the big picture in the chapel itself: therefore had to manage from sketches ; and to sketch the oblique perspective correctly, without one jot of knowledge of perspective, was not easy.   I sat and looked at the background until I was sure of the direction of its lines.   Strange to say, my eye did not mislead me, and every man in the picture, front and back, found his correct place in the composition.   Well, it could hardly be called a composition, as the upper half of the picture was all architecture, the middle line of the canvas a dense mass of heads, after which followed a row of hands, then a row of legs, and finally a row of boots.   It had no beginning and no end; it was a section of the chapel congregation *cut* out.

About the end of February the picture was far from finished, and my struggle was going on.   I was un-doubtedly breaking down, and there was only another four weeks before "sending-in" time.   Whenever I re-turned to Bushey there was trouble to settle.   Every-thing was in a chaotic state, and left for me to put right. The poor parents had been badly dealt with, and the servants were up in arms at some injustice or other done them.   I put everything down to the delicate state of the wife's health, and tried to make peace all round, after which I wearily returned to town.   I now found I could not stand to my work.   I lost my appetite, and also felt perpetually drowsy, which I took to be a bad sign. The picture *must*, at all hazards, be done for that year's Academy ; but how ? I was a total abstainer, and would not dream of taking alcoholic stimulants. Somebody said I needed exercise. But I had not strength for that ; still, the remark struck me as being right, and the question only arose as to *how* I could combine exercise with my work.

I heard of a "machine," invented by an American, that had saved many an overworked brain in that busy country, and was called the "health lift." I knew of *one* that was in England, and I immediately bought it, and brought it to my studio. A strange-looking machine— not covering more than two feet of ground, with some queer levers in it, and two handles sticking up. It is so arranged that you can measure precisely the weight you pull, from a few pounds to twelve hundred. And, strange to say, you pull yourself up, and yet your own weight is cunningly deducted. One pull seems to stretch and affect every muscle of one's body. I took a light weight first, and then increased it day by day. A pull was easy to take between my work, and so I persevered until my strength returned ; and this happened in a marked degree in eight days, and I was a new man in a fortnight, the work never having been interrupted.

The picture was finished, and sold to the man who had bought many of my water-colours, for £1,200. This left me but little surplus, as I got into debt during my wife's illness. I had little hope of its being hung well in the Academy, in spite of the good opinion of all who saw it in the studio. In those days there was not this fashionable Show Sunday, when every beginner sends out cards promiscuously, hoping there will be a squash. So I had but a few friends to see it. George Richmond, R.A. (kindest of men), came to see it on the recommendation of somebody. He said he liked it, and said he would try and hang it well, as he was one of the "sworn hangers," but remarked that he had only one voice in the matter.

My own disappointment in the picture was that it was so utterly *unlike Walker*. Strange fascination for my beloved master!—a master by choice, for I never met him personally. I had so short a time in which to paint the picture, that I *had* to do the heads and coats broadly—and this was my salvation. This picture emancipated me from Walker, although my love for his feeling of Nature remains strongly ingrained to this day.

A week after sending the picture to the Academy, I received two letters, one from Sir Frederic (then Mr.) Leighton, and the other from Mr. George Richmond, expressing the enthusiasm the picture evoked in the Council, of which they were members. Mr. Leighton's letter was full of praise and kind wishes. I was an entire stranger to him. Mr. Richmond wrote that they all clapped hands as the picture was brought before them. The unexpected triumph did not touch me more than the kindness of these two men in writing to me, a young outsider, and these two letters will always belong to my most precious possessions.

The opening day happened on a first of May, and all the papers burst forth in praises of this picture. It was undoubtedly something new. I met Pinwell in the

Gallery, who said, " *You have done the right thing at the right time.*" This was my aim. But I owed my success to my obstinacy in the choice of subject. Here was I, not yet twenty-five years of age, with a dazzling art career opened out on one side, and a black cloud of sorrow hanging over me on the other.

At this time Miss Griffiths paid us a visit, and saw our chaotic house. The wife pleaded hard for her help, which ended in this self-sacrificing woman promising to give up her career as nurse, which promised to be most successful, and throw in her lot with ours. My parents rejoiced, for they had an intense admiration and love for her already, and felt that I could go to my work *un-harassed,* as a strong hand would be able to keep matters right in the house. Alas! it needs but little strength to upset many lives. Thus it proved that the weakest person in the family had the most power of upsetting everything. All that was built up was pulled down by this one effort. Her good and her happiness was our combined thought, but all our efforts proved futile. The old condition came round again and again. My work was constantly interrupted, and Miss Griffiths' ceaseless efforts to keep matters right fell helpless before this strange disintegrating power of the invalid wife.

There were now two children, the last a girl. My mother could not endure the life here any longer. She said, " I cannot see my son's unhappiness, and his use-less struggle ; and as I am helpless, like all those around, to prevent it, I will ask father to take me to Germany, that we two may live peacefully together in our old age."

O

Their old age! Yes; it was my dream to sweeten *that*, and now, I thought, I have embittered their last days. Let anybody who loved his parents, and had done his utmost to make them and everybody about him happy, feel for a moment what my grief was at this decision. I *did* get them to postpone their departure, hoping—oh, the hoping!—that matters would mend before long. A younger sister of Miss Griffiths was now asked to come to us, to see if *more* help, of such loving and self-sacrificing help, could not mend matters.

However, in '78 the parents left us, and I made them a home in Landsberg am Lech, Bavaria, very near to where we all were born. Now came the Paris International Exhibition. I was most anxious to exhibit there. As an outsider I was permitted to send two pictures (the privileged ones could send ten pictures), and my 'Chelsea Pensioners' of course must go. But the owner refused; it was not until the greatest possible pressure was put upon him that he consented.

Hardly had the picture been hung but its notoriety commenced in Paris. There were ten medals of honour given to the Art sections of the whole world, awarded by an international jury, who wrote down the names of the painters they thought entitled to the honour. I received the largest number of votes, and stood at the top of the list. A fortnight after this decision, Fildes and another friend came down to Bushey to visit me. I met them at the station, and the moment they got hold of me, they commenced to congratulate me most violently. I could not understand, having heard nothing about this matter, because nobody from the Academy had informed me. "Yes, you and Millais," they said, as they pulled me about afresh.

I was not an Associate of the Academy when this distinction came to me, a distinction that immediately carried my name to all parts of the world, as it did for other recipients—Munckacsy, of Hungary, Wauters, Belgium, and so on.

In the years '76, '77, '78, I produced, in spite of all difficulties, some large pictures for the Academy : 'At Death's Door' (Bavarian) ; 'Eventide' (English) ; and 'Der Bittgang' (Bavarian). My chief object in doing German subjects was to strike out in a new vein, fearing to be "ticketed" all my life with the one article which had been successful. I lost favour in the eyes of the public, who fully expected me to paint nothing but Pensioners for the rest of my life. But it secured the freedom of my career. On this action I look back with much satisfaction. And now, in '78, with the 'Pensioners' so much to the fore, a strong stand for artistic freedom was still more necessary. Fortunately I had a foil already at the Paris Exhibition, as my other oil picture was 'After the Toil of the Day.' I also had two water-colour drawings there.

To turn back a year, I must mention two important matters—the painting of Richard Wagner the composer, and my starting etching. Wagner was an object of great fascination to me, and his visit to England was hailed by me as a great chance to paint him. I told the members of the German Athenæum that I should give *them* the portrait if they got him to sit to me. Wagner, in a way, promised to sit, and allowed me to visit him

daily. I was also supposed to make notes at the rehearsals in the Albert Hall. I resented this method,
but there was no help for it. Wagner would not
sit, and my friends did not want me to give up the
portrait.

A month of this shilly-shallying nearly drove me to
desperation. He did not know my work, and did not
care to find out. He permitted me to be about him, as
he would a harmless dog. Never was my spirit of independence so tried, and I felt that an end must be put to
this sort of thing. So on the Friday morning I determined to try what *sheer* memory would do, and set to
work on an imperial sheet of paper, as I preferred to use
the water-colour vehicle for such an experiment. It grew
I know not how. The next day I worked still harder
and more excitedly, and finished it before the evening,
having had nothing to help me but my memory. On
the Sunday I took it up to town and showed it to
Wagner. He was amazed, and said, " Sie hexen ! " (You
use witchcraft). His entire manner towards me changed,
he became affectionate and highly appreciative. His
remark about the picture was, " Yes, I like to look like
that." Then he gave me a sitting for a quarter of an
hour, and all I did was to correct the drawing of the ear.
The contrast of his expression and the expression I had
on my portrait was almost ludicrous. I had painted an
expression that indicated emotion, and there sat the
real man, smiling and pleased, which had the effect of
shortening his upper lip, drawing down his nose, and
lengthening his chin. I preferred *my* Wagner. The
picture is still highly appreciated by the family, and

considered the best portrait of him. It hangs in Mrs. Wagner's house at Bayreuth.

Etching opened out a new channel of interest to me. This new art was taken up by me with feverish enthusiasm, and was acquired in the way in which I seemed destined to acquire all knowledge, viz. : first, to *do* a thing, and *then* find out *how* to do it. I blundered through it somehow, and erred principally on the side of size. No plate could be too large to start on. There seemed nobody at all willing to give me any information either, and beyond Hamerton's book I had no guide.

But all through my life I preferred to find out things for myself, and in my *own* way too. Before I was half shown a method of work by some practitioner, I would, by intuition, know some other way of doing it. Continuing this egotistical narrative, I may add that the itch to try a thing before sufficient knowledge of it had been gathered has characterized my whole life. It has its drawbacks, but it has given me the power of immediate expression in whatever art material I choose to express myself. Mine is essentially a life of action, of doing, of making and producing. This did not originate in me ; it already existed in our family two generations back. Enthusiasm, and the power of imbuing others with it, has helped me to carry out so many of my plans. Defeat I do not acknowledge (even if others proclaim it), because I look beyond, and see always some success looming in the distance. High spirits and hopefulness are the two points in my organization that have helped me through so many wretched hours of sorrow. But enough of this.

About this time I did much indifferent work ; it was hurriedly done, and not always good in subject. I had an arrangement with Goupil's for the sale of my work, and the temptation to hurry work was brought about by my perpetual arrears. By the advice of Miss Griffiths it was now arranged to borrow a lump sum of money to pay off the debts, then to live most economically, keeping strict account of all the outgoing money.

The borrowed money was paid off in instalments in three years. This saved us, although it brought with it some peculiar anxiety. It was lent me by a man professing to be my best friend, but who nevertheless had the loan registered, and took as security a bill of sale on my furniture—my father's handiwork!

In the autumn of 1878 my high spirits gave way, my health broke down under the yoke of sorrow, and I fell prostrate with brain fever. Miss Griffiths understood the symptoms, and prevented me from suffering more than I did by her skilful and timely nursing. The doctor gave her no little credit for what she had done. For six weeks I could not use my eyes, for the light was unbearable. This illness coming on my Paris success, the world said I could not stand it. Kind world! How little it knew!

When I recovered, the first serious work I did was the water-colour portrait of Tennyson, for which I stayed at Farringford, where I received much kindness from that angelic lady, his wife. I was much in need of it, as I was only convalescent. My meeting with the great poet was characteristic, and ought to be recorded. It took much motive power to bring us together, and to get his consent to sit.

I arrived late, and having left my luggage at the hotel, made my call at the house. Hallam Tennyson first greeted me, and said a few kind commonplaces to me. Presently the door opened, and the old poet came in with his head drooping. I advanced to him, and we shook hands. His first words were, " I hate your coming ; I can't abide sitting."

It was not a promising beginning, but after some conversation he said he would send for my luggage. This was a step in advance. The conversation was kept up on general subjects for an hour or two—*not* broaching the subject of the portrait however ; and I went to bed with grave doubts in my mind.

Hardly had I commenced to undress when there was a knock at the door, immediately followed by Tennyson peeping in. He did not enter, but said from the door : " I believe you are honest ; good-night." He shut the door, and certainly left me to cogitate over the strangest reception I ever experienced.

I found him always an unwilling sitter, but received only the most delightful courtesy and kindness from all, and I shall not easily forget the long walks over the downs, in all weathers, with this great student of Nature.

The year 1879 was full of incident. I was prepared to try a new scheme for landscape painting, which was to combine romanticism, comfort, and rest, with healthful activity, to culminate finally in a large landscape. I soon fired my friend, Mansel Lewis, with the same desire, and we proposed to go together, camping on my principles. Our tent was sixteen feet long by eight feet wide, with four plate-glass windows (out of which I could see my landscape), double canvas for the walls, and an extra fly-sheet for the roof, and boards for the floor. The servant was one of Mr. Lewis's keepers, and occupied a smaller tent. The spot (selected by Mr. Lewis, who knew Wales) was some distance from Capel Curig. We arranged all as comfortably as possible, but the stove *would* smoke, and the messenger with food and letters *would* be late. In after years we had petroleum stoves that acted perfectly in all weathers. I think we felt *all* the "sensations," and rather more at times than we expected from this first experiment in camping out. There I produced a landscape called 'Windswept.' But painting, living, and sleeping in the same tent did not answer well, and I determined to invent a hut for future painting purposes.

Now came a commission from King's College, Cambridge (on the strength of my 'Pensioners') to paint a portrait of Lord Stratford de Redcliffe. This was my first commission for a portrait.

In June of this year ('79) I was elected an Associate of the Royal Academy. Miss Thompson, now Lady Butler, ran me so close that I only got in by one vote.

I visited my parents at Landsberg in July, and noticed an indefinable change in my mother. She did not care to go with me and father to Ramsau, but preferred to stay in Landsberg. I painted a large oil colour landscape called 'God's Shrine,' and a large water-colour called 'Grandfather's Pet,' also some small oil pictures. This

work was a trial to finish, as I fell ill three weeks after
we arrived, and did not get really right until our return
to Landsberg, where I spent some time—some very
happy time. That was the last time I saw my mother.
When saying good-bye at the station, I noticed how
keenly she felt the parting.

In November I painted John Ruskin in water colours.
I intended now to make a collection of portraits of
celebrated men, and this was the first. These I leave to
my children.

The day before Christmas Eve a letter came to say
my mother was ill, but as it was not considered dangerous, I was not to come. On Christmas Eve a telegram
came, saying she was dead. The doctor could not well
define the cause of death. But I knew well enough ;
and it is not the first woman of her temperament who
has fretted herself to death. She had told Miss Griffiths
that the sorrow of my home had broken her heart, and
that her thoughts could not be got away from it. She
hardly thought about my successes ; the mother only
thought of the son. Death was not needed to make
this woman a saint. . . . I bought the house in
which she died, and the ground about it. Next to
the house, which I have kept intact, I have built a
monument to her memory in the shape of a romantic
and habitable tower, over one hundred feet high,
which I call " Mutter-thurm." Her portrait is set in the
carved panelling of the principal room. May this tower
serve to tell all who see it of the love I bore my dear
mother.

My father now returned to me—alone. I made him

a nice room to work in, and he gradually learned to bear his grief in the love we all showed him.

The next year ('80), about April, we camped in that desolate spot, Lake Idwal, and this time my father also joined us. He had a tent of his own, and his romantic nature enjoyed it immensely. The new painting hut proved a success. It was 11 feet by 8 feet, with one side glass, and turned on a pivot, being made fast by four ropes. This could be erected where the subject was, and could be placed on any piece of ground that size. Nor was any piece of it too heavy for one man to carry.

During the ten weeks I produced a wild, desolate landscape, afterwards called 'The Gloom of Idwal.'

In this year I started mezzotint engraving, another art I was compelled to find out for myself, as engravers do not tell their *secrets.* On the strength of this it was a satisfaction to hear from Sir John Millais that he considered my engraving of his 'Caller Herrin'' the best thing ever done of his work. He especially alluded to the face. I know of at least *one* engraver who made a wry face at this remark.

My picture, 'Missing,' was painted this winter, and mezzotinting and etching went on apace.

In the following year ('81) we camped on the same spot again, but this time the party had increased to ten. The subject I selected to paint necessitated the erection of my hut over the river—which I managed by planting it on planks of twenty-four feet long that spanned the river. Although the river rose one foot higher than I had allowed for, there was no damage done. The storms that are so prevalent in the spring months in Wales never removed a single peg of our tents, or did us any mischief.

My landscape this year was called 'Homeward,' and was the first into which I introduced a figure.

A couple of portraits were again commissioned to me, and I seriously thought of giving more attention to this branch of art. To further this object I asked Archibald Forbes to sit for me, and my portrait of him made its mark in the Academy. Many men who were pleased with the manly bearing of this interesting man, said to themselves, "*I* would like to be painted like *that*," and straightway came to me for their portraits. Of *course* I made them *all* like Archibald Forbes!

I now gave my whole time to portraits, and my artistic friends commenced their cry of shame! Frank Holl was similarly attacked. It is strange that so many subject painters despise portrait painting. Verily I believe no man would be guilty of such an opinion if he *could* paint a portrait. Is it not true that we admire the portraits of the old masters beyond all things? Just because portrait painting secures a more certain income than can be expected from subject painting, painters of the latter class of art are able to accuse portrait painters of turning their thoughts only to money-making. It is a base accusation—as false as it is ridiculous. The successful and much-sought-after portrait painter finds his work most arduous, as he is destined for months each year to have two and three sitters—and sometimes four—a day.

The portrait painter truly records history. His art is

understanded by the many, whereas subject painting is for the few. Nor is there a more priceless possession in this world than a good portrait of a relative. Fie upon the affectation that pretends to despise this great art !

In November of '81, the doctor that my wife consulted, strongly advised her to spend the winter in a warmer climate. It was decided she should go to Wiesbaden. Miss Maggie Griffiths consented to go too, provided my boy went. This broke up the family. My boy cried himself to sleep night after night at Wiesbaden, longing for home, and the expected health never was obtained. That summer we all met at Ramsau, where I painted a large water colour of six feet, by five feet, with life-size figures, entitled, ' Life, Light, and Melody.' It was a *tour de force*, which was well received in the Grosvenor Gallery the following year.

New domestic arrangements were agreed upon, as my wife had taken a fancy to a doctor who was going to move to Vienna. Thither she wished to go, and it was arranged that Miss Maggie Griffiths and both children should accompany her, because I had planned to go to America with my father ; but he was unwilling to go unless Miss Griffiths came too.

My journey to America was a great change for me, and prevented my domestic trouble from again seriously affecting my health, which was much shaken.

Soon after her arrival in Vienna, my wife took a severe chill, which struck again to the lungs. I received daily telegrams from the doctor, who constantly urged me not to come. Miss Griffiths' brother went over, at my desire, to help his sister ; and his letters, written always with the desire to spare me pain, carefully concealed the truth from me, but at the same time gave rise to doubts in my mind about my wife's real condition. On Miss Griffiths' advice, we broke the suspense by suddenly taking the first steamer to England, intending to go straight to Vienna. At Liverpool another brother of Miss Griffiths met me with the news that my wife was dead. We then all three went direct to Vienna, and heard the terrible truth why we were kept in suspense. Her condition had been beyond our help, so the doctor took the responsibility of keeping us away. The brain had quite given way, and galloping consumption had done the rest. What Miss Maggie Griffiths went through in nursing my wife in that last illness she alone can tell. Our presence seemed to make them all, children included, feel as if *they* all had been brought out again from the tomb.

Our life began anew at home. Under Miss Griffiths' management there was splendid order in the house, and the interesting plans were completed for building a great house here in Bushey. Miss Griffiths, with the help of her sister, watched over us ; the children became strong again, and lost the scare that was upon them ; and my father was happy in the thought of this house being built, into which all his work would go. In order to expedite the work, I had a number of wood working machines sent from America. But above all things, I had persuaded my Uncle John (my father's youngest brother, who had remained in America) to settle over here, and help us to build the house. He came over with his family to settle in Bushey, where his son Herman was already an art student partly under my care.

It is now necessary to speak of the founding of my art school, which happened about this time in this wise. A neighbour of mine in Bushey, Mr. T. E. Gibb, was guardian to a friend's children, and amongst them was an art student. He put out feelers to know if I would teach her. I said, " No," as I could not teach one alone. Going up to town one day with Miss Griffiths, he spoke to her of this matter, and it was she who suggested he should build a studio in Bushey for art students, whose work she was sure I would criticise. He declared himself only too ready to do this if he thought I would give my time to the scheme. I was then consulted, and readily agreed to design and run the schools, taking the responsibilities of all the art matters, if I were left free to act without restraint of any kind.

And this I would do without any fee. Mr. Gibb, being a man of business, could not understand *why* an artist, who has risen to some eminence, should care to give up valuable time to teaching without remuneration. But he found me firm, and agreed to build a large building with the accommodation that I had planned, for a maximum number of sixty students.

During my absence in America the building was erected, and was finished by the time I returned. Our first term commenced October, 1883. A code of work and a code of behaviour was printed for the guidance of the students, who mustered to about twenty-five the first session, as it was my plan *then* only to take them for a nine months' session. Being absolute in power, I was able to alter the rules at any moment, when I found they did not work well. And this nine months' session was soon altered, for it debarred many students from coming to the school at all. All art schools of note of the present day have traditions that block the way. They have committees and councils that hinder experiments, and impose on the students the folly of competitive prize work, to prove the efficacy of the system of teaching. I had but to go back to my student years to know precisely the kind of teaching that would be best for students. On this experience I have based the system of teaching at the " Herkomer School."

A great many difficulties presented themselves at the outset. The social difficulties were all settled and directed by Miss Griffiths, who likewise fixed the price for the lodging-house keepers, and helped and advised them in furnishing their cottages for students. I can safely say that the splendid moral tone that now exists in the art colony of Bushey is principally due to her guidance and help at the beginning of the scheme. It was all so new for the place and for the students. There is no art school in the world, in a country village, which is yet within easy reach of a great city, and this novelty in itself brought about some difficulties at the outset, but has since proved to give my students at once the advantage of a figure and a landscape school. My fears lest the good students would leave me were soon dispelled, and I found them most anxious to settle around me. I built the first five studios for the first successful students who had graduated out of the school. Studios of this kind have increased rapidly—some being built by me, and some by the students themselves. And as I write now, in October, 1889, I can declare the colony, with those who study in the school, to contain over one hundred of my adherents and disciples. The formation of this school, and its successful working, belongs to the best, and certainly the most useful, things I have done in my life.

I have also established a school of engraving that is highly successful. Engraving is work that these young painters can do for the sake of an artistic livelihood until they can devote their *whole* time to painting. It is no small matter for a young student to get £450 for a single plate, which is the price of a commission just obtained by one of my students. A great deal of work is put into my hands to distribute amongst the struggling students, and this in itself is an advantage that was denied us as students. Thus it will be understood that there is a condition of things existing between master and pupil which cannot be found elsewhere in modern times. Miss Griffiths at the very commencement started the Sunday receptions in my studio for the students and their friends. On these days I would exhibit the work that I had in progress, giving the students in this way the most valuable lessons.

But to return to the narrative of my life.

In the spring of '84 I camped once more, with Lewis and my father, not far from Portmadoc, in North Wales. The landscape that I produced this year was bought by the Academy for the Chantrey Bequest Fund, and was called ' Found.'

On the 12th of August, 1884, I married the lady who had been our best friend—Miss Griffiths.

A spell of unutterable happiness was thrown over me, and for the first time in my life I felt what it was to have a wife. I thought I knew her well, but good women, strong-charactered women, seldom show their real nature until they wed a man they can love.

My whole life changed. I altered so much that my friends exclaimed, when they saw me, that I looked ten years younger. But it seemed as if my cup of bitterness was yet to be kept full; and had I chosen to see the cloud that was slowly but surely gathering around our happy life, I might have lost the bright hours that healed me after my long years of suffering. The truth, the fearful truth, was forcing itself upon us, that my wife had heart disease. She knew it, but was too brave to let it interfere with her thoughts or her work. Rheumatic fever when a child had given a predisposition that way; but the strain of all those hard years in my family did its inevitable work on her constitution.

During the winter of '84 and spring of '85 I painted my first lady portrait of importance. It was done at the instigation of my wife, who urged me not to allow myself to be twitted any longer by the sticklers, who declared I could only paint men. I chose the youngest daughter of my friend Mr. Owen Grant. This portrait of Miss Katherine Grant—ordinarily called the 'White Lady'—has become so celebrated that I need say little about it.

Endless verses were sent me to send on to her; stories and fabricated biographies were written about her by the dozen.   I heard the picture mentioned at hotels, and even in the trains on the Continent.   At Berlin the only chairs in the Exhibition were placed in front of this picture—it was Miss Grant, Miss Grant, Miss Grant! Many offers of purchase were made to me, two, strangely enough, from two gentlemen whose daughters were supposed to be the image of my Miss Grant.   But I painted it for myself, and it was not for sale.   Its success, first in the Academy here, then in Berlin, then in Vienna, and Munich, was indeed striking.   There was for a long time an irritating obstinacy about many people who believed there was only one Miss Grant, and that was the well-known American lady of that name.   This section was equally split in two : one said it is the General's daughter, the other section said it was Miss Adele Grant, who was once engaged to an English nobleman.

I had the satisfaction of looking back upon striking successes in subject pictures, in landscapes in portraiture of men and of women, and, added to this, some considerable success in etching.

Now came a communication from Oxford, asking me if I were willing to accept the Slade Professorship, should I be elected.   I willingly agreed, on condition I should be left entirely free in the choice of my lectures.   I told them I knew neither Latin nor Greek, but professed to be able to express in simple language the thoughts I had evolved from my work.   That was precisely what they wanted, they said, and I was accordingly elected in the summer of 1885.

I appreciated this new field of action most sincerely,

Professor Herkomer, M.A.

because lecturing was no trouble to me, but was often an intense pleasure. Its origin lies in this fact : that the moment I can *do something*, I wish to tell others how to do it. You remember I had this tendency as a boy, and have it now still more intensified. It is this gift that makes me love teaching, and every lover of teaching, if he have but a moderate power of expression, must long to lecture. I had been lecturing for some years in many parts of England, and with much success. I am never nervous, and can say what I have to say *better* to a large number of people than to a few. A lecture never fatigues me, but, on the contrary, the sympathy I always get *back* from the audience fills me with an elixir of life that I crave for if I have been too long without lecturing in public. My professorship at Oxford gives me the opportunity of concentrating my " Talks on Art."

We now made plans to go to Germany, that I might carry out an experiment of painting some forty pictures in the Alps, to be exhibited by themselves at the gallery of the Fine Art Society, in New Bond Street. But in the summer both my wife and I were in need of a little change, so in July of that year, '85, we decided on visiting a town in the north of England, where we could be quite quiet and enjoy a little rest. One day my wife was looking in a shop window in one of the narrow streets, while I made a purchase, when she happened to see a child under the feet of a horse. Without a thought for herself, she darted out into the road, caught up the child just in time to prevent the wheels from running over it. All this was the work of an instant, and by the time I accidentally looked up, she was carrying the child to the pavement. That same night her own child was born—prematurely and dead! The shock killed it, so the doctor said.

Some three weeks after this, when the wife was strong enough, we returned home. She had given a life for a life!

We soon made arrangements for our journey to Ramsau, and we arrived there on a Sunday, unpacked our things, and finally arranged the new studio that I had built there for the express purpose of painting this series of pictures. Our spirits once more ran high, and we all seemed delighted to be there, especially my father, and the visit promised much happiness. This promise lasted but twenty-four hours, for the very next day my wife's sister, Maggie, was attacked by diphtheria. Quickly my wife rearranged two rooms we occupied, sent for carbolic acid, and prepared for this dangerous illness. She and the invalid were shut off from the rest of us for a fortnight. This cloud removed, we once more breathed, completed our visit, and returned home with my forty pictures—some quite, and some not quite, finished. But as the private view was to be in November, it was a great strain to get them all ready.

Between this came my inaugural address at Oxford, which took place in the Sheldonian Theatre, before a large audience. This address, contrary to my general custom, was carefully prepared. At its conclusion, the Vice-Chancellor, Dr. Jowett, made a speech in which he welcomed me to Oxford in terms I shall not easily forget. Two fresh honours came to me now in rapid succession, the degree of Master of Arts, and of an Honorary Fellow of All Souls College, Oxford.

Let me hurry over events now. The Bavarian pictures were finished, and we had a private view of them in Bushey for the friends and neighbours about us. That was on a Saturday. It did not seem to fatigue my wife to receive so many friends, and she was able to go to town to dine at a friend's house, where we met many notable people—H. M. Stanley, General Wolseley, Archibald Forbes, and many others. My wife never was brighter than on that evening. On the Monday I went up to town again, to arrange the Bavarian pictures in the Gallery; but could not get finished, so had to return on the Tuesday. On this day I returned home a little late, and arrived at Bushey Station at twenty minutes past seven. Here I was met by our doctor, who took me by the arm and said, "Mrs. Herkomer is very ill; I wish to prepare you for it." I arrived home, and saw by all the faces that crowded in the hall that it was not illness but death! That day my wife had been entreated by her sister to stay in bed, as she had had many attacks of pain in the heart, and seemed weak. Whilst she was giving directions to her sister for the management of the children and the house during our proposed absence in America that winter, she said, "I feel as if I were going to faint," and immediately fell back dead.

It was only that very day that one of the most eminent physicians in London, who had recently examined her, wrote to say she would run no risk in going to America. There was no room for despair on my part, for the terror-stricken family needed all the support I could give it. And this strength was mercifully given me until I arrived with my father in New York in December. There I fairly broke down. Once more, as in those early days, my father sat by my bedside, nursing me through a desperate night of fever. But friends soon mustered around my bedside ; and American friends *are* friends indeed !

When strength returned I started my portrait work in Boston. This wonderful country, with its great and good people, has certainly had its effect upon me. The spirit of enterprise, of daring, and of self-reliance of that nation greatly worked upon my imagination.

My future house took shape in the hands of that truly great architect of Boston—H. H. Richardson. He evolved an elevation on my ground plans (in itself a great feat) which ought to mark a new era in architecture in England. It was just this elevation I could not do well enough myself, and in exchange for his work I painted his portrait.

I also painted, during this visit, a companion picture to the ' White Lady ! '—but this time it was a *black* scheme ! It happened that soon after I arrived in Boston, I saw a lady who seemed to me very beautiful—older than Miss Grant, but of a fine, intellectual type. I found her willing to sit for me, and I painted a picture that has had, amongst artists, a greater success than Miss Grant's portrait.

During this visit I painted an immense number of portraits, and both my father and I found the touching kindness of these people take off the first terrors of our sorrow—my sorrow! Alas! how could I ever get back confidence in life—in happiness? Now came over me an almost maddening desire for perpetual work—so as not to think of my life—only work, work, work.

My sister-in-law directed all things, silently and sweetly, and administered to our comforts. Although she had never taken responsibilities into her own hands, she immediately rose to the occasion when called upon to act.

When I returned from America, on the 25th of May, I found equally hard work awaiting me here at home. I was glad, and longed to keep up the strain—anything to ward off the risk of becoming embittered. My children, my students, my work, my father—all seemed to save me from myself. That I overworked was certain, and who could work, as I worked, and not suffer? I painted thirty-four portraits in 1886. This included some gift portraits, and some that were painted for myself.

My father's health began seriously to fail now. He could not walk well, and could no longer work at his bench. It was a bitter thought to him to have to stop work, and he still hoped he would get better; but I clearly saw the beginning of the end, and it added another heavy weight to my already overburdened life of sorrow.

The following year ('87) I undertook, in spite of so much portrait work, to paint forty water-colours of scenes around my home for another exhibition at the Fine Art Society. Who will not wonder when I say that many and many a day that summer did I rise at four in the morning, and go out sketching until seven ; then take breakfast, and catch the eight o'clock train to town ; paint three sitters there, and return in time for an evening effect in Bushey ! I hungered even for more work, for some new excitement ; and sure enough in the autumn of this year it came unexpectedly.

My boy casually asked me one night if we could act some piece that Christmas. Certainly, and in the studio. On reflecting, I found this would interfere with my work. I possessed on my property, adjoining the house, a small building that had once been a chapel. Some students were painting there. I proposed to decorate this room as the auditorium, and build a small stage to it. But, like so many of my plans, it developed into an important undertaking, and the decoration of that small hall took much longer to complete than I had bargained for. On Christmas Eve it was finished, and the stage nearly ready. But the piece ? I had arranged with a friend to write me a bright piece for which I would try and compose music.

Music now took a strong hold upon me, and I longed to compose. Musical themes kept coming into my head, and I wrote them down as suitable for certain scenes that were in my mind. The promised piece was not forthcoming, as my friend had other work to do. But here was a theatre, with a stage, all in readiness ; only the piece was wanting. Nothing daunted, I started a fragmentary play myself, wrote it out in scenario form ; then wrote all the music for it before I had any words.

Two songs arrived from my friend, who, however,

had not even the story settled ; but I found I could fit them into my fragment. I selected some words from George Éliot's ' Spanish Gipsy,' and *fitted them to the music ;* the words that were still wanting I did myself —such verses !

It was a medley,—fragmentary, weird, and romantic. It had no beginning and no end. But it captivated all our friends. On the advice of my late friend, Mr. Levy, of the *Daily Telegraph*, the press was invited, and was warm in its appreciation. The scenery was new: I invented a new sky, a new kind of moon, and abolished footlights! I changed—with perfect truthfulness to Nature—the night sky to dawn. I could not write dialogue, therefore I determined to have as much as possible in dumb-show, with the accompaniment of characteristic orchestra music. This put me on the track of a new kind of entertainment.

My sister-in-law was the sorceress, and the rest of the characters were taken entirely by ourselves, *i.e.*, the school and my family. I took the part of a blond shepherd, and I can safely say that my dance in that character could not be equalled by any other member of the Royal Academy ! We invited nearly a thousand people to the eight performances of the ' Sorceress.'

Although I composed the entire music, I did not score it for orchestra, but gave that over to a musician, whom I paid for the work. I soon felt that this method was a mistake, and determined for future operations to do it myself, feeling sure I could master the technical difficulties of instrumentation. As it was, I had indicated throughout how I wished it treated in the orchestra.

Now I saw that such an entertainment could be made an annual or biennial festival for my pupils and myself, I determined immediately to invent another piece—a story of quite a different character, a story of English village life of the 14th century. I wrote it out in scenario form, and placed it in the hands of Mr. Joseph Bennett for the lyrics.

The ' Sorceress ' was performed through the months of April and May ; and the rehearsals—which were often daily, but always when they did not interfere with the school work—commenced in February. During this time I had to finish my forty water-colour drawings of ' Scenes Around my Home,' for the Exhibition which was to open in April, and had to paint portraits without intermission. How I lived through all this work I cannot now understand. I was under a false excitement, and feverishly kept it up to crush a longing that was beginning to overpower me, the longing for domestic happiness.

The play was an intense enjoyment to my father, who was present at every rehearsal and every performance. But he was now fading, and I suffered, as only a son can suffer when he sees a parent he worships die gradually before his eyes.

My sister-in-law had gone to her parents in Wales with the children for a much-needed change ; but I had to go on working at portraits, without the chance of a rest.

The end of my power of restraint had arrived, and I felt I must change my life or fail to carry out my work. It meant breaking down utterly and irrevocably. I wrote to my sister-in-law, and asked her to be my wife —at the same time urging her to return, as my father was getting rapidly worse. She came, and brought me the answer, and with her "yes" came life to me. When the children heard of it, they clung to her and devoured her with kisses. When my father was told of it, he said, as well as he could through his tears, that he was now happy, he had so wished this. When my pupils heard of it, there was universal rejoicing!

One night, towards the end of July, my father seemed brighter, and was carried to bed with positive happiness upon his face. He slept until a quarter to eleven, and when he awoke, he complained of a little pain in his shoulder. His attendant, seeing a change in his face, knocked for me, and as I arrived he was breathing his last; his jaw dropped into my hand. Then, and not before, did his beautiful colour leave his face. There he lay, looking kingly in his death! He was a king; he was, and is, my idol. No child could have longed for its mother more than he longed for me when I was absent. Years ago he said to me, "We now change places; you shall become my adviser, my parent, and I will be your child." This was our relationship. I worshipped him, and that is all I can say.

Yet suddenly the burden,—the *whole* burden of sorrow had dropped from my shoulders, and the storm of my life was over. Peace—enduring, blessed peace—I saw before me as I stood by that deathbed, with my future wife at my side.

In August I took my boy abroad, and arranged all matters for the wedding. Determined to leave no question as to the legality of my marriage I became a German subject, and so freed myself from the English law that forbids union with a deceased wife's sister. This was not difficult to accomplish, seeing that I am a German by birth. The Mayor of Landsberg arranged it all for me, and also made me a citizen of Landsberg. So I am now again a German subject, residing in England.

The family had now all arrived at Landsberg. The mayor, on the night preceding the wedding, came with a double quartet of singers to serenade us, and made us a short speech of welcome, especially mentioning me as the youngest and greatest citizen of Landsberg, "unser jüngster und grösster Bürger."

On the second of September we were married in my own tower, with the mayor to officiate ; and a more solemn, beautiful ceremony I could not have wished for. It took place in the principal room of the tower, where the portraits of my father and mother looked down upon us. As we left the tower for the house, next door, music (the 'Lohengrin March') seemed to be in the air, for I had secretly placed ten of the best brass instrument players from the Munich opera house in the uppermost storey of the tower. The effect of this was magical. Various selections of music were played for an hour, and then we drove off for a short honeymoon. We rejoined our family in time to return to England before my school opened in October.

Our front door at home in Bushey had been garlanded by the students for our return, and "welcome" seemed to meet us everywhere.

A week after our return I put into shape a large
subject picture of the 'Charterhouse Chapel,' which I
had failed to do during the previous six years.   I never
could tackle it, but now it found immediate expression.   This picture was exhibited in the Academy,
1889, and was bought by the Council for the Chantrey
Bequest,—the second time I have been honoured in
this way.

The new Pictorial-Music-Play was already begun before I left for Germany.   I worked steadily at the music
every spare moment through the winter of '88 and '89.
I only worked in the evenings, or on dark days,—the
exception being a day, now and again, when I needed
rest from painting.   My new stage was finished, with its
depth of forty feet, and I started my scenery in November, for which four carpenters and my smith were
retained.

I soon found that writing for orchestra was an excitement and a delight well worth the trouble it gives.   I
doubt indeed if scoring for orchestra can be acquired
if it does not come naturally.   To me tone-painting
seemed like the pictorial art.   I had no lessons in it,
but studied the technicalities of the instruments from
books.   I studied the scores of the best composers, then
made a plunge for it.   It was not very likely that I
could wait long after it was finished before I heard it in
some form a little more audible than I had been hearing in my mind for months.   So I tried it with the
string band only, with my friend, Joseph Ludwig, as
leader ; having the wind instruments played on the
piano.

But the want of a conductor was soon felt, and so it happened that I was forced, willy-nilly, to use a batôn for the first time in my life. How I puzzled those poor musicians! But I saw clearly enough that I ought to be able to conduct, and was glad to take Mr. Ludwig's offer to teach me " how to conduct." I practised under his tuition; the piano, and the first violin played by himself, was my orchestra. Now I could do it I felt sure, and soon had the full band down to Bushey for a complete rehearsal, with choruses and solos, but without scenery or action,—merely to try the music in concert form. I conducted this rehearsal with full enjoyment to myself and satisfaction to the musicians. I know of no excitement so intoxicating and so fascinating as conducting an orchestra that plays one's own music.

A copy of the score was now sent to Vienna, to Hans Richter, who had promised to conduct my performances. Asking Richter to conduct for me was a bold step, because I knew he disliked amateur work; and curiously enough, some four years ago, after inspecting the many things that were going on in my home, he had said, half jestingly: "One thing, dear friend, I beg you won't attempt, that is composing; leave that to us musicians." I said I had no intention at all of sinning in that direction. I spoke the truth at the time. From the earlier pages of this book, it will be readily seen how I drifted into composing music. Gradually the play took shape, as our rehearsals, which were always in costume, took place three and sometimes four times a week through April and May. The scenery, with its variety of effects, was all finished, and rehearsed with my six men who were trained to work my lights.

Richter was surprised when he saw the scores, and the moment he came to Bushey and saw my scene, threw himself, heart and soul, into the scheme. He rehearsed the choruses afresh, and rehearsed the solos. He threw a singular charm over all he touched in this way, and nothing can describe the security we felt in him as conductor. It was particularly striking, as we had had such dreadful experiences the year before with a conductor who simply beat time like a metronome. Richter carefully watched the actors, and, as he saw they were getting faster or slower, as it might happen, he would regulate his orchestra. This orchestra was composed of twenty-seven picked players from Richter's London orchestra, and many soloists, with Joseph Ludwig as leader.

To the nine representations of 'An Idyl' we invited some 1,500 people, and then we gave three charity performances for our Village Nurse Fund.

The play was a signal success, and there was but one opinion about it. Actors, musicians, artists, theatrical managers, and public were alike interested and pleased. The guests were all taken into the studio and round the workshops after each performance. I had a few professionals on the stage, but otherwise my students were the actors. And all was entirely under my control and direction.

After the last orchestral performance, Richter brought all the musicians on to the stage, and took me aback by making me a speech in his and the orchestra's name.

He said he was prejudiced against my music, as he could not believe a man already so proficient in one art could turn to another with success. But all his feelings changed when he saw the score. And continuing, he said, among other things: "That first rehearsal, gentlemen, was a surprise to us all. His music is never commonplace, and nearly always *original.* I am sure I express your ideas too, when I say I hope he will continue in music, as we shall look forward to his next work with the greatest interest."

Memorable, indeed, were those 'Idyl' days for us all. One extra performance we gave for our villagers, who had shown their keen interest in our proceedings by decorating the village street with flags.

The following document of thanks, signed by them all, is worth noting here :

To Professor Herkomer.

" Dear Sir,—

"We, the undersigned inhabitants of Bushey and neighbourhood, beg respectfully to return our most sincere thanks to you for the great privilege we have been enabled to enjoy, through your kind invitation, of seeing the performance of your pictorial music play, and inspecting your marvellous workshops and beautiful grounds, not forgetting Mrs. Herkomer's kind hospitality.

"We acknowledge, with gratitude, that it was, for this village, a most fortunate day when you became a resident amongst us, and we sincerely trust that both you and yours may be long spared ; and we

wish you most heartily, good health and a continu-
ance of prosperity.

"We are, dear Sir,

"Yours respectfully."

[Here follow the signatures.]

As I write this, on the 20th of November, 1889, in
the midst of my family, with my boy and girl, already
helpful in so many ways in the home, and proud and
happy in the possession of the baby brother that lies,
just two months old, in the identical cradle my father
made for me forty years ago, I look at him, with his
likeness, already so striking, to my father; at his sweet
mother, radiant with joy; I see my house growing
apace, and my colony of students around me; and my
existence is summed in the two words: Peace and
Success.

Charles Hallé

Sir Charles and Lady Hallé.

SIR CHARLES HALLÉ is one of those extraordinary organizations, to whom nothing seems difficult, and who can do serious work, good work, and never appear hurried, when dozens of other men would be tired out. Doing, without exception, that which he does well, he is with regard to quantity, as well as to quality of work, phenomenal. I am happy to say that I was able to compile so many details of his early life and his career in Germany and in France, that I imagine this biographical sketch to be in all likelihood the most complete ever published about this remarkable man.

The grandfather of Sir Charles Hallé was a manufacturer, and his son, the father of the present Charles Hallé, made himself a musician, though, as Baron Rothschild said of Thalberg, he didn't need it. He was organist at Hagen, a small but lovely town in Germany, where he arrived in 1817, and remained to his death, 1848. He was the founder of the so-called 'Gesellschaft's Concerte,' which are still now in existence. He must have had a remarkable aptitude for music, for he played concertos on the flute, on the violin, and on the clarionet. Being organist, piano was self-understood. His son, for whose impartiality I must not absolutely vouch, mentions even a sweet tenor

voice, which enabled him to sing very successfully
Beethoven's 'Adelaide.'

His must have been rather a rare organizing talent
if he could, with the amateur society which he had
created, give such compositions as oratorios by Beethoven, Spohr, and Haydn.   He seems to have been
a man both of very genial humour and large-hearted
at the same time, because those who wanted amusement and those who needed protection flocked readily
to him.   He married in the year of his arrival (1817),
Miss Caroline Brenschedt.   She was a most amiable,
charming, and talented girl, the daughter of a judge,
and nearly related with several well-known aristocratic
families, Fürstenberg, v. Hügel, etc.   I have seen a
portrait of her when she was eighty, and even at that
age you could easily detect the traces of a most attractive expression, of great intelligence, and a tender
heart.   It was her musical talent, both as a singer and
pianist, which first influenced her little son.   She had a
younger sister, who married Gustav Harkort v. Har-
korten, the well-known director, one might say creator,
of the first Saxon railway, to whom grateful Leipzig
voted and erected a statue.

The 11th of April, 1819, was a Sunday, and an
Easter Sunday; and with the first morning bells was
announced the birth of a baby, weak, and barely
thought strong enough to live, and yet that baby is
to-day in his seventy-first year, six feet high, straight as
an arrow, of great physical and mental force, and on the
eve of a journey to Australia, where he will remain tour-
ing with his illustrious wife until October.   That under

the care of his tender mother he learned how to read and write when five years old is not so surprising as the thorough knowledge which she imparted to him of the musical notes and their value when he was barely three years old. Not only all he learned and knew later on, but his very existence, is due to the never-relenting care and anxious watching of his mother. Where in the world should we look for love in its purest self-sacrificing abnegation, if not in that inexhaustible treasure of tenderness, a mother's heart?

The little man seems to have made, under the loving tuition of his mother, such progress, that his father had to be appealed to, who first wrote him small pieces religiously preserved in a red leather book; but by-and by the execution growing more advanced, papa Hallé wrote for his young virtuoso a sonata which the child at the age of five performed at one of the subscription concerts, standing, not seated. That is now sixty-five years ago, and such was the impression produced on his youthful mind, that he wrote part of it down for me only a very short time since. Imagine the sensation such an event produced in a town which at that time had barely 5,000 inhabitants. Little Charlie, however, continued studying seriously, and at the age of seven, accompanying his father to Cassel, where the famous Dr. Spohr then lived, he played with such success before that great man, that he was compelled to give a public concert, supported by two of the greatest singers of that time, Sabine Heinefetter and the tenor Wild. In this concert he played variations by Ries, and some of Henri Herz on a *motif* from 'Joseph,' extremely difficult; in one of the latter, the *motif* is given in jumps of two octaves, first for the right then for the left hand. The success was prodigious, and it must be said, to the great praise of his father, that notwithstanding the numerous pressing offers of engagements held out by enterprising *impresarios*, he refused all, fearing that the nervous strain and the unavoidable "spoiling" would unfavourably influence the serious artistic development of his son. Only in the subscription concerts, which were more like a family affair, he played, and the list of pieces there performed included a number of solidly difficult works, by Ries, Hummel, etc. I say solidly difficult, because those were not mere show pieces, but they required a pianist of solid cultivation, who knew his scales in thirds and sixths, and his left-hand practice well. Moscheles' 'Alexander March and Variations' would now not be tolerated in a concert room, yet they were at that time considered one of the great test pieces. We now arrive at his ninth year, when he practised his alto voice in the Singverein, and was appointed accompanist. Influenced by his father's versatility, he learned several instruments, flute, violin, and that usually underrated, yet so important instrument, the tympani. Being there continually either at the piano or in the orchestra, he learned, we may say, intimately the scores of a number of classical and sacred works, and so made himself a thorough musician.

About that time travelling companies arrived frequently at Hagen to give performances—some dramatic, some operatic. They all came naturally to Mr. Hallé to beg his chorus and orchestral assistance, which he always conceded, although it was mere favour, payment being out of question. Some short time after, when little Charlie was eleven years old, just when the orchestra was wanted for such a performance, his father fell ill, and the boy, as if that was a self-understood thing, asked would he be allowed to conduct, which was accepted, as an additional attraction ; and sure enough, he conducted the 'Zauberflute,' ' Freischütz,' 'Preciosa' (Weber), ' Fra Diavolo,' 'Maurer und Schlosser' (Auber), etc., deriving the greatest benefit from the practice of reading orchestral scores. The habit then acquired proved invaluable, when, after I might say a lifetime, he took the bâton again at Manchester. Having been taught harmony and counterpoint since his sixth year, he contracted the dutiful habit of composing every year a little piece for his father's birthday, which by-and-by grew even to the dimensions of a concert overture. Having made progress on that most kingly instrument, the organ, and having learnt all that it was possible for him to learn at home, he was now sent to a school where the clever private tuition of his mother proved so useful that he became at once the second of his whole class, including the highest studies. His love of music, however, prevailed over all, and as in the little town there was no regular music-seller, and he could not even buy music-paper, he took to ruling ordinary paper with staffs, and patiently sat down to copying Beethoven's sonatas, and in this way write for himself a library of classical works. I cannot pass over a very remarkable trait of abnegation on his father's part.

Charlie, who had been a weak child, suddenly got the measles. Of course his mother nursed him night and day ; yet once when she had retired to rest, relieved by his father, the fire, which of necessity had to be kept up, had gradually gone down so low that when the father remarked it, frightened that the child might catch cold, and no wood being in the room, instead of losing time by going downstairs and finding fuel, he took his flute, quickly decided to cut it to pieces, and threw it on the dying embers, and so contrived to maintain the warm temperature.

One of the gifts necessary for a musician, although not every musician possesses it, is a very exact ear. Mr. Hallé's friends often amused themselves with putting the little fellow with his face to the wall and making him guess the notes they touched on the keyboard, and when he got victoriously through the trial, they touched sometimes most fearful discords, only to see would his sharp ear penetrate the chaos, but he did. I said just now that this is a gift not within every musician's reach. There was Adolphe Adam, one of the most graceful and celebrated composers of France ; he could not for the life of him say what was the chord he heard on an instrument, and I remember that on one occasion an organ-grinder drove us all wild, when he turned to me and said : "He plays in B, doesn't he ?" "No," I said, "he plays in E," which was about as far away from his guess as it could well be. I will, however, say that I know another French composer, yclept Berlioz, who had not only the most correct but the most nervously sensitive ear that I believe any human being can have. I saw him

once at a rehearsal jump down from the conductor's desk
and pounce upon the clarionets, shouting out, " Brigands,
you are not in tune together." And they were not ;
but he had heard the small difference through the din
of the whole orchestra.

The studies lasted until the boy was fifteen years
old (1834), when his father decided that both for his
piano-playing and the development of his studies in
the scientific part of his art, he must go to a more
important town, so as to get higher tuition ; for, be it
well understood, music consists of two distinct parts, the
art, which wants inspiration—inborn genius, and the
science, which wants study to master the rules. This
explains why so many musicians who know all the rules
—for study everybody can—are not great artists, for the
inborn talent has nothing to do with acquirement.

It was therefore decided that with a letter of introduction by the great organist, Dr. Günther, the young
man should go to Rinck, at Darmstadt, one of the most
esteemed theóricians, and the composer of even now
famous works for the organ. This great musician so
befriended the boy that he soon became one of his
most industrious pupils. And there you will see a Continental notion : he took his lesson from six to seven in
the morning, when Rinck had done his first hour of
composition, which gives you an idea of his early rising.
I remember when in Vienna, and wishing to see Hans
Richter, who lived about six miles away from me, he
told me : " You'll find me at home nearly every day until
nine o'clock in the morning." Anyhow, the study of
counterpoint, fugue, and composition were gone through

conscientiously and thoroughly during two years, a
further element of help being found in Justizrath Gott-
fried v. Weber, whose 'Theorie der Tonkunst,' a most
important work, had long been young Hallé's musical
bible. With the year 1836, however, the father thought
the time had come to send his son for the highest perfection in his piano playing to Paris, to the then world-
wide known Kalkbrenner. But then Kalkbrenner had
by that time given up teaching, while Hallé, introduced
into great banker families, had many opportunities to
hear the great pianists of the time—Liszt, Thalberg,
Chopin, each of whom impressed him deeply in his own
way. He progressed, developed and increased his talent,
as every man of real talent does, by his own observation,
and by listening to those from whom he had anything to
learn. That is Paris ? At any rate that was Paris. If
you go there to stare in the shops on the Boulevards, or
the jewellers in the Rue de la Paix, or if you make acquaintance with the fast men, or for the matter of that
the fast women, you will pass your time very quickly
and after a few years have wasted your hopes, your
inclinations, your character. The real Paris is that of
art and science. If you are happy enough to get into
the right set, to know the celebrities, *les grands hommes,*
then you may be sure that your time will be profitably
and delightfully employed. Republics may be the highest
development of political principles, but in our days
science and art want the patronage of court and patri-
cians. Never shall I forget the *Soirées du Louvre* which
were given by the Comte de Nieuwerkerk, when everybody who was there was somebody—Rachel, Ingres,

Gustave Doré, Auber, Gérard, Arago, Roger, any artist of
repute, great poet, great singer. By the side of the painted
galleries were these living galleries, and what could we
see and hear there! Alexandre Dumas père, who in his
boasted quality of Republican never frequented court
circles, had the most delightful parties. Often people
asked him : "What did you do,—had you music?"
"Never," he said, "*nous avons causé.*" But in order that
such *causerie* should for hours interest you, those who did
causer had to be of a very superior order. At Halévy,
too, were wonderfully interesting parties. *That* was *le
vrai monde de Paris,* and into a similar world, fifteen
years before, came Hallé. Now he must have been of the
right stuff, because though it is comparatively easy with
a good letter of introduction, etc., to enter the enchanted
ring, you must show that you are somebody to maintain
yourself in it. Young, enthusiastic, full of talent, he
worked some ten or twelve hours a day, which is much
easier said than done, and although I who write these
lines have once in my very young days practised fourteen hours, because it was the day before my first concert, I would never advise anybody to go that length,
because in nine out of ten cases it will result in fatigue
and weakness of the wrist, and would have done me the
same harm had not the excitement of the moment made
me do what two hours afterwards I could do no more.
Sir Charles tells me that he sometimes had his hands
quite swollen, yet he persevered.

Until then, viz., during the first year, the kind father
furnished the sinews of war, which enabled his son to
devote himself entirely to the study of the great mas-

ters, and perfecting himself. Being of a very amiable disposition, and having a great knack for languages, he soon made acquaintances, connections, which ripened into friendship ; and when he then expressed a desire to have pupils whom he could teach, what was then rather rare in Paris, sonatas by Beethoven, he very soon saw himself surrounded with pupils as eager to learn as he was eager to teach them. Small pay to begin with brought larger terms by-and-by. His income received various support from his being appreciated by some great amateurs as performer, and notably one great *agent de change*, Mons. Guibert, offered him very acceptable terms for performing every Thursday night in his house, only for the family circle, the best music inclusive of the Beethoven sonatas, which at that time were not so well known in Paris. This engagement lasted for six years with the utmost regularity, and the circle of his friends and patrons enlarged accordingly. Then he made the acquaintance of Salvator Cherubini, who was one of the higher employés in the ministry of home affairs, and spoke so highly of Hallé's performances to his father, the famous composer, that it was arranged between them to introduce Hallé to the old gentleman. Fancy his joy on learning that, when a boy of eleven, Hallé had conducted Cherubini's 'Watercarriers,' and knew the whole score by heart. Cherubini soon took such a fancy to the young German that he received him at his *soirées intimes* on Sunday evenings, when before him and a few friends Hallé played Beethoven's sonatas.

He then made the acquaintance of Heller, Berlioz, and other European celebrities. Through them Heine and

Wagner came to see him, and his modest apartments in the Rue Laffitte became soon the rendezvous of such a number of great men that at last he was urged to overcome his modest shyness and enter the public arena, which he did with Allard and Franchomme, at that time the greatest violinist and 'cellist of France. Laurels and sovereigns were the pleasant result of these concerts, but there was one thing which he ardently desired, and which seemed of nearly insuperable difficulty, viz., to play at the Conservatoire, where Habeneck, with an iron will and great artistic superiority, had introduced the symphonies of Beethoven, which he rehearsed for years and performed with a perfection which it will be very difficult for any orchestra on earth to surpass. But Hallé did not know Habeneck; he was a very great pianist certainly, but not known enough to venture on such a demand, when the most curious accident, without his seeking, suddenly brought the fulfilment of his ardent desire. He walked home one night through the Rue du Helder, humming to himself a tune, when an old gentleman who walked before him stopped, looked at him, and walked on. Hallé, never even taking any notice of the gentleman, moved on and hummed on, when suddenly the gentleman turning round stopped short before him, and said, " Vous chantez la neuvième?" (You sing the Ninth Symphony.) " I do," said Hallé. " But who are you?" asked Habeneck; and late at night, in the street, the acquaintance which he so much had wished for, ripened into the friendship which led afterwards to Hallé being invited to play Beethoven's E flat Concerto at one of the concerts of the Conservatoire, thereby giving him what the French call the *baptême artistique de Paris.* That so many admirers and influential friends introduced him to other great people, and that at last Paris became that paradise for him which has proved so attractive for many people, is easy to understand, but— the paradise was not to last.

The delightful circle of friends, including Armand Bertin (through Berlioz), Lamartine, Ary Scheffer, Ledru Rollin, etc., was attracted to his house since he had married Mdlle. Désirée Smith, of New Orleans, and was thereby in every sense enabled to receive. The concerts with Allard and Franchomme had by-and-by acquired such popularity that the hall was every time filled— George Sand and Chopin in one box, Guizot in another, then M. Lamartine, and many others. The Court had invited Hallé on one famous occasion, when Queen Victoria visited Louis Philippe at the Château d'Eu, and everything seemed most promising, when down came the crash of 1848! The 24th of February sent the royal family out of France and became the signal for the revolutions of Berlin and Vienna. There was for a long time no hope for art—the concerts were empty, the pupils and their families emigrated, nobody knowing whether the Revolution of 1848 would not, like that of 1789, be followed by a reign of terror, and nothing remained for young Hallé but to seek the refuge and patronage which a neighbouring country offered.

Hallé went to London, where he met not only a number of friends from Paris, but a number of English friends whose acquaintance he had made in Paris. Chorley and Davison, who held the sword of musical criticism, and

Ella, who gave the best classical concerts with his quartet, forming the musical union. Invited to play at the Covent Garden Theatre Concerts, and at Ella's, having met Guizot, who then lived in Brompton Crescent, and whose daughter took at once piano lessons, he was on the point of making his nest comfortably in London, when the brother of a banker whom Hallé had intimately known in Paris, persuaded him to come to Manchester, where certain favourable conditions insured his peaceful artistic life. He was there, in 1850, appointed conductor of the Gentlemen Concerts, one of the oldest societies in England, and after having established chamber music concerts, for which he engaged all the great performers from London, Molique, Ernst, Vieuxtemps, Sainton, Piatti, etc., he gave, from 1857, his great orchestral concerts; and has since then passed the winter in Manchester and the summer in London. He conducted German opera in Manchester, and English opera (with Sims Reeves, Santley, Parepa, etc.), in London. For the last four years, he conducts the Philharmonic Concerts at Liverpool, and is notwithstanding his seventy years a most active, busy man. It is well known that many years ago he became the professor of the Princess Mary of Cambridge (Princess Teck), of Princess Beatrice, of the Princess of Wales, with all of whom he remained a *persona grata*. How much his recitals have contributed to propagate really good music through the whole country everybody knows, and it remains only to give the date of 1857, when the great loan exhibition in Manchester took place, when he was empowered to engage a powerful and numerous orchestra, the concert performances of which were received with such success that he retained the orchestra, gave a regular season of fifty concerts per winter season with them, and through continual training, rehearsing, and intelligent guiding, brought them to that degree of perfection of which they gave such eminent proof during the London season of this year. That the Queen, in recognition of his great merit, conferred the well-deserved honour of knighthood on him we all know. This has not prevented him from continuing the simple-mannered, courteous, obliging man, who, with German thoroughness and sincerity, is a perfect English gentleman.

His first wife having died rather young (some twenty-four years ago), he has since married the great violinist, Madame Norman Neruda, who when six years of age electrified the Vienna audiences, created as a young girl quite a *furore* at Paris before the most distinguished audiences, and is now in London the most honoured leader of the Popular Concerts. Joachim, before she arrived here, said to Mr. Hallé : " I recommend to your attention this young lady. Mark my word, when people have heard her, they will not think so much of me." Volumes have been written about the immensity of her talent and the grace and charm of her execution. I only regret, knowing her as I do since her childhood (her sister having studied in Vienna under the same professor, Fischhof, as I did) she would not give me any details sufficient to write a proper sketch of her life, so full of distinction of every kind ; and all I can do, is, to wish Sir Charles and Lady Hallé a happy journey, a glorious sojourn in Australia, and a speedy return to their numerous friends in England.

Josw Hofmann $\frac{1}{8}$ *1887*

Three Prodigies.

YES, three prodigies, of whom one is eleven, the other thirteen, and the other—forty-seven; and it is equally miraculous to see what the one can already do with eleven, as what the other can yet do with forty-seven. Not to speak in enigmas, let us proceed to giving the names of each of our heroes, of whom, by the bye, one is a heroine. The youngest of the *sancta trinitas* is little Josef Hofmann, as cunning a little rascal as you can imagine. He is a prodigy; not like those overforced hothouse plants who stand no wear, and with whom the real prodigy was only the youth, so that youth gone the prodigy was gone, and nothing remained. Little Hofmann has not only the vivifying spark, that spark which Prometheus tried to steal from Jupiter, but he has, besides his astonishing performing talent, a decided great talent for composition. I am less surprised by his improvisations; they are flimsy and only superficial glitter, vastly inferior to what an English boy ten years ago did, whose improvisations were really interesting. I speak of Eugène d'Albert, actually a very young man, but recognised one of the greatest pianists, and travelling at this moment in America with Sarasate, receiving for his winter tour ten thousand pounds.

Little Hofmann, ætatis four, begged a piano from his father, and when his father refused, he said, " Not many months will pass when everybody will reproach you with having denied me an instrument ;" and six months afterwards he had it.   He was left to himself to study, though the father gave him occasional advice ; and what was his astonishment when, after one year, the boy told him he knew all the usual exercises, and was so anxious to write music that he actually presented his father with à mazurka, his own composition.   He then made his way, playing in public when he was six years old, and it' is said, although I will not vouch for the fact, that Rubinstein, speaking of him, said, " Wonder children as a rule become no artists ; but I have heard this boy, he is a wonder, the like of which the history of music has never known before."   I doubt this, because young Filtsch, who unfortunately died at thirteen years of age, a pupil of Liszt, and another name not quite unknown to history of music, viz., Wolfgang Mozart, were quite unknown to Rubinstein.

‘ The sensation which the little boy, a Pole, father and mother being Poles, produced in America, whence he was brought away, his nervous system giving way under the overwork, leads me naturally to speak of his rival, Otto Hegner, who is, I believe, one year older, by far more solid a pianist, a straightforward German nature, without any fuss or intrigue, or any of those little tricks Josef Hofmann plays in public. Otto Hegner knows, like a thorough artist, only one aim, to do full justice to the composer he has to interpret, and to please the public by playing as well as he can. But publics in

Otto Hegner 11/10/89.

general, and Americans especially, wish before all to be
amused. What is the piano to them ? The whole world
plays the piano well. Hans Richter, the great chef
d'orchestre, said once to me: "But, us poor conductors
excepted, everybody plays the piano splendidly." If
listening to a pianist be an amusement, how happy would
Londoners be during the season. It is certainly most
remarkable that a boy so young as Hegner should play
so well, but then he is in good health an ordinary thing ;
he plays correctly, an honest but uninteresting affair. He
knows none of the little *minauderies* and *coquetteries* of
his little rival, and consequently he does not amuse the
ladies. Little Hofmann comes before the public with a
solemnity, and bows like a master of the ceremonies, as
serious as a gravedigger, which has in itself a most
comical effect. Then, when he is at the piano, suddenly
he pulls out his handkerchief and wipes the keyboard ;
then all the ladies giggle, and thus he is altogether
such a finished little coquette, against whom a natural,
straightforward boy like Hegner has no more chance
than an unaffected woman would have against a scheming
coquette if they were both bent on conquering the same
individual.

Perhaps you will now allow me to mention to you
the third prodigy, a little girl whose portrait at seven
years you see, and who at that age was put upon
a table, *coram publico*, and sang by heart words and
music of all the airs, at least of very many, she had
heard her mother sing. That the child was not one of the
prodigies who deceive those who hope in their future,
that the child did become somebody, and that the antici-

pations for an artistic career were realised, will be sufficiently answered by the name of that child—Adelina
Patti. A child may be wonderful for memory and
quick learning, or it may without great study overcome
difficulties which another child not only would want
double time to get over, but which it would perhaps
never learn at all. But Adelina Patti is a wonder in this,
that she not only did all she astonished the world with
without any study whatever, but that she is now, at forty-
seven years, the same wonder-child, because all that she
does now, like all she did as a baby, comes to her by
nature. She sings like a thrush, a lark, a nightingale.
This century has certainly seen the two most remarkable—and by positively opposite methods remarkable—
singers: Jenny Lind, with a voice so obstreperous
that when she came to Paris she was told by one
of the great singing masters there to return to her
country (Sweden) and marry some respectable young
man, for a singer she would never be ; and Adelina
Patti, who stood before the public before she knew how
to read, singing *una voce poco là* with all possible and
impossible fioritures, without one lesson. Jenny Lind,
who had the most unimpeachable purity of intonation,
who made shakes that any instrument might envy but
not imitate, had by hard study, great intelligence, and
most uncommon perseverance, bent and subdued a
perfectly rebellious organ ; and Adelina Patti, who sings
as pure as a bell, trills like a lark when it rises to
invisible heights, and having no more trouble in ac-
quiring it than in learning how to speak French, Italian,
Spanish, English, German, not having had either a

À Monsieur Louis Engel
Souvenir amical (7 years old)
d'Adelina Patti Nicolini

Donsond Phᵗᵒ.

lesson in any of these languages, and speaking them not only fluently and entirely with the *génie de la langue,* but with such an accurate accent that the Spaniards call her Spanish because in the Calle del Fuente she was born ; the Italians claim her most reasonably, because she is born of Italian parents, her mother, La Barili, having been a singer of repute ; the French consider her French, as the wife of a Frenchman ; the Americans even say she came there as a child, was educated there, developed there, became a great singer there, and they do at any rate the most generous thing, they pay her more than anybody ; and when last year she opened the Auditorium, Chicago, and sang, " Home, sweet home," nothing but this song, she received £800 for singing less than eighty notes ; that is to say, for the thirteen notes composing the first part of the melody, £130.   She has with all that the inborn grace and that charm which creates such a magnetic attraction with the public, so that whenever she is announced to sing at the Albert Hall, she fills it, and she alone can do it.   Her beauty, her voice, her talent, her charm, all is born with her. She has only to take the millions which people are but too anxious to offer.   And one should think that having everything that the sweetest triumph, that of vanity, can wish, the most costly presents every day arriving at her residence from rich friends, and sometimes from quite unknown people,—having everything and every- body at her feet, one should think that she must be the happiest being on earth.   I cannot say that to my know- ledge she is.   I fancy she feels bored ; the homage and the diamonds and the flatteries, lasting now for more

R *

than thirty years, seem monotonous. She is in the position of the King Polycrates, who could have no misfortune, for like that *gourmet* in Paris, who had thought out the most refined *menus* and eaten the most *recherchés* dinners, and was suddenly advised by a poor man for once to dine off a black radish (a vegetable unknown here) and a piece of brown bread, and enjoyed that more than a dinner at the Frères Provençaux. So do I honestly think that if Madame Patti could meet for once in her life with some creature, male or female, who would *not* do what she wants, would not be too happy to guess all her desires, would not treat her to the titles—which she has heard *ad nauseam*—of Queen of the Song and Diva, and what other nonsense, but would have skill and tact and superiority enough to tyrannize her, I fully believe that that person she would adore. She accumulates her wealth because people force her into it, but to my mind she is utterly *blasée*, having had all that the most profuse Providence could grant her, she has nothing to desire, and everything that is brought to her, or offered her, has been offered a hundred times before. She seems to me to stand alone on her pinnacle of fame, and to lack that which constitutes the blessing of social life—a circle of sincere friends.

THE END.

INDEX.

247